I have had the privilege of meeting r
stand out as game changers, which is he.
Nullmeyer. When I first met him over 40 years ago, I sensed that he was a special person. His confident, friendly manner and mile-wide smile told me that I was in the presence of a unique and gifted individual. As I got to know him better and watched him in the pulpit and working with others, I saw a man who didn't just love God but adored Him.

Ernie lives and breathes the Word of God and delights in its revelation. He is an extraordinary communicator whose command of the written and spoken word has helped him to witness for his Lord so powerfully for over 60 years. Whether as a radio broadcaster, a preacher, a pastor, a family man or a friend, Ernie has always had two hands in the air reaching up to God and those same two hands reaching out to those in need. As the leader of the Barrie and District Christmas Cheer Association for nearly 30 years, Ernie lived out his faith, helping thousands of less-fortunate men, women and children to celebrate Christmas with food on the table and toys under the tree. He led an army of volunteers to create a living, breathing testament to the words of Jesus *"Love your neighbor as yourself"* (Matthew 19:19) and showed how much he cared for others through sacrificial service and selfless commitment. Rightfully earning the nickname "Mr. Christmas," Ernie helped spread joy and hope to people who were lonely and in need of help, a position he well understood, as he would often reflect on his own boyhood memories of his family receiving assistance when they were in a time of financial difficulty.

Our pastor recently preached on the theme "Healthy voices in your life accelerate healthy choices in your life." When I think of the people that God has brought into my life, Ernie Nullmeyer is one of those healthy voices, helping me to make wiser choices. His buoyant enthusiasm, consistent witness and unquestionable integrity have encouraged me to grow in my faith and commitment to our Lord. God has blessed this man with many wonderful gifts, all of which he has invested wisely through his many years of Christian living and ministry, which you will discover for yourself as you read this book. Ernie has dedicated his whole life to putting into practice the spirit of the two greatest commandments: "Love God and serve others" (see Luke 10:27).

**Jeff Walther**
**Long-time Broadcaster**

## MY TRIBUTE TO ERNIE NULLMEYER
## A MAN BLESSED OF GOD

As you look back in retrospect
You have much in which to rejoice
For all the blessings from our Lord
As you made Him your choice.

God has been faithful through your years
He's blessed you with so much
He's used your "gifts" in manifold ways
So many other lives to touch

You've been such a great blessing
To many along the way
Being a pastor, friend and guide
Knowing just the right words to say

You've left an imprint on many lives
You've been a mentor and friend
May God reward you continuously
Until your earthly journey ends.

Written for my favourite pastor and friend

**By Jean Anderson**
**(nee McDonald)**

As a young boy, Ernie Nullmeyer was "bigger than life" to me! One weekend my parents took me to Barrie to visit my grandparents, who attended Emmanuel Baptist Church where Ernie was the pastor. On the Sunday, we all attended the worship service at Emmanuel. I had never been in a church where the service was broadcast on the radio. I was fascinated by it all—and more so by the complete sense of peace that Ernie had as he welcomed the radio listeners and entered into his sermon.

He was an amazing preacher—his strong voice and evident sense of confidence in what he was speaking about spoke volumes about him as a person and orator. He had this great smile and a twinkle in his eye that conveyed a great love for the Word of God, his parishioners and his radio audience.

I could hardly wait to get back to Barrie, simply to hear Ernie preach. As I shook his hand upon departure, he made me feel so very welcome and valued. While there were further visits, the next moment of deeper memory came when

Ernie took on the role of conference director at the famed Canadian Keswick Conference on Lake Rosseau in Muskoka. I had a similar role just up the lake at Keswick Youth Camp. Our friendship intersected on many occasions. The enterprise was challenged financially, which had significant impact on our leadership at many levels but more so for Ernie and his family than for me. His dependence upon God and his patience during very stressful moments impressed me deeply as a younger leader and have carried on to this day.

As the years have gone by, we each have faced trying times and changes in our leadership contexts. Once again, Ernie's approach to life—to serve God fully and humbly and to be a blessing to others—has challenged me to bask in God's presence and to allow His Spirit to touch each moment of my day and in turn to be a blessing to others.

I am so thankful for Ernie's mentoring example over these many years.

**John H. Wilkinson D.D.**
**Chancellor, Tyndale University College and Seminary**
**Executive Coach and Strategist, Youth For Christ Toronto and Canada**


"Young man," the preacher asked me, "what would happen to you if you met death tonight?" These words burned into my heart on May 24, 1954, I as sat in a Christian youth rally, listening to a 25-year-old dynamic preacher by the name of Rev. Ernest Nullmeyer, the pastor of Emmanuel Baptist Church in Barrie, Ontario. I was 17 and had been in trouble with the law and living a rather reckless and purposeless life.

Neighbours of ours who had recently become Christians through the ministry of Pastor Nullmeyer invited my mom and me to go with them to a service at Emmanuel. My mom wanted to go and persuaded me to go with her. The first thing that amazed me was how many youth were in attendance, and the second thing was how young and dynamic the preacher was. At the service Pastor Nullmeyer encouraged the youth to attend an upcoming out-of-town youth rally at which he was to be the guest preacher. It was Pastor Ernie's inspiring and passionate preaching that inspired me to attend the youth rally, where I realized my need to accept Christ as my Lord and Saviour, which I did that day in May 1954. Through the exemplary life and teaching of His servant Pastor Ernie, God transformed my life forever.

Pastor Ernie encouraged me—with only a grade 8 education—to go to Toronto Bible College (now Tyndale University and College), which he had graduated from. There I graduated with a bachelor of theology. He has been a sterling role model for me for 62 years and also a spiritual "brother" and "father." My own father took his life when I was three years old.

Pastor Ernie is a man of God with an amazing knowledge of God's Word, which he articulates with great clarity and passion and lives by daily. He is also blessed with a wonderful infectious sense of humour through which he blesses many each and every day.

**Fred Campbell**
**Retired Missionary to the Philippines and Social Worker with Children's Aid Society**

# HOW I
# TRIUMPHED
## OVER MULTIPLE TRAUMAS

WITH A
**SMILE** *on My Face*
**SPARKLE** *in My Eyes*
**SPRING** *in My Steps*
AND
**SONG** *on My Lips*

## A MESSAGE OF HOPE AND INSPIRATION

# ERNIE NULLMEYER

**How I Triumphed Over Multiple Traumas With A Smile On My Face, Sparkle In My Eyes, Sping In My Steps And Song On My Lips**
Copyright ©2017 Ernie Nullmeyer
All rights reserved
Printed in Canada
ISBN 978-1-927355-21-3 Soft Cover
ISBN 978-1-927355-95-4 E-book

Published by: Castle Quay Books
Tel: (416) 573-3249
E-mail: info@castlequaybooks.com | www.castlequaybooks.com

Book design by Burst Impressions
Printed at Essence Publishing, Belleville

**Cataloguing in Publication information may be obtained from Library and Archives Canada.**

Dedicated to my beloved son Kevin
who completed his earthly journey
and commenced his eternal journey
August 9, 2010

*"I will go to him, but he will not return to me."*
(2 Samuel 12:23)

And to my beloved grandchildren,
who keep their grandpa "young in spirit"

SAVANNAH, CAITE
ASHLEY, ANDREW, JOCI, ALI
BROOK, TAYLOR
KYLA AND LILY

*Only be careful, and watch yourselves closely so that you do not forget
the things your eyes have seen or let them fade from your heart
as long as you live. Teach them to your children and
to their children after them.*
(Deuteronomy 4:9)

# PROLOGUE

Often when I am out and about and people discover my age and see evidence of how unusually healthy I am in my eighties, I will get asked something like "What is your secret?" My response is always "I don't know if there's any secret to it, but I do have three principles and seven pillars that I live by, and of course a little good fortune is involved as well." As time is usually of the essence when I am asked that question, I decided it was time for me to put into print those principles and pillars that have enabled me—in spite of many traumatic experiences—to enjoy a healthy, joyous life.

I say "in spite of" because it's easy to look at someone like me who has a sunny, effervescent, insouciant approach to life and assume that the person has never had any bad experiences to deal with. I guess the old cliché is appropriate here: "You can't tell a book by its cover." Often after I have preached a sermon on the subject of pain and shared a number of my painful experiences, someone will say to me on the way out, "I always assumed you hadn't had any painful experiences." You see, it's not so much *what* we have to deal with in life but *how* we deal with it that matters!

That is what this book is about. Life is a long, winding, uncertain road, and none of us knows what's around the bend for us; nor in many cases would we want to know. I'm sure we can all agree that "The greatest certainty in life is uncertainty" (a Nully Nugget).

Readers may wonder where that designation "Nully Nugget" originated. I had the pleasure of having five Dutch sisters work for my decorating company, and when new employees would come on board, they would often ask, "What should we call the boss? Shall we call him 'Reverend' or 'Mr. Nullmeyer' or what?" The sisters got together and decided that my new title and nickname would be "Nully," and I liked it. The "Nugget" idea came from my son Kevin, who had a master's degree in marketing and was always full of great new ideas. I liked it, and it stuck.

Speaking of my beloved son Kevin brings forth another reason I have written this book. Kevin often urged me to put my Nully Nuggets into print and also to write a follow-up to my memoirs. He would say, "Dad, you have had a lot of losses in your life, and yet you just keep on smiling and singing. I think that writing about those losses and yet coming through them without being bitter would be a great inspiration to people." I thought for a long time about taking Kevin up on his advice but kept putting it off as I knew it would take an incredible amount of time and energy to write a book that I could be proud of and people would want to read. I just kept mulling around in my mind what the title of the book would be and what the structure would look like.

And then came the moment when I sat down at my computer and commenced putting my thoughts into words. That moment was about a week after family and friends had gathered to celebrate Kevin's life. That very sad story is related in part 1, Traumas Revealed, chapter 5, "Loss of My Beloved Son." I kept asking God, "How am I going to get over this one?" And then the answer came loud and clear into my mind and spirit: "Start writing that book Kevin talked to you about and dedicate it to him."

So one morning—bright and early, following breakfast and my exercises—I sat down at my computer and prayed, "Lord, through Your Holy Spirit, guide me in every word I should include in the book, so that it will be an inspiration to all who read it."

Little did I know back when he suggested it that my dear Kevin would never get to read the book he so passionately encouraged me to write. However, he has been with me in spirit throughout the writing of the manuscript, and I know that he will be looking down from heaven with that wonderful smile he so often had on his face, pleased that I took his advice.

The third reason I decided to put my thoughts in print is because since my youth I have desired and tried to be a blessing in some little way to everyone who comes across my pathway. I want this book to be a blessing—in some little way—to everyone who reads it.

My desire for you—as you read the book and as you live out your life—is beautifully and poignantly expressed by the apostle Paul in his letter to his fellow believers at Rome: *"May the God of hope **fill** you with **all** joy and peace as you trust in him, so that you may **overflow** with hope by the power of the Holy Spirit"* (Romans 15:13, emphasis added).

May your life and mine be not just filled *"with all joy and peace"* but overflowing with that joy, peace and hope! Overflowing *to bless others*! Amen!

# INTRODUCTION

I have divided the book into two parts. In part 1, Traumas Revealed, I share some of the major traumas I have experienced in my life. This is not for the purpose of trying to gain pity but rather as a lead-in to part 2, Traumas Relieved, with the hope that my experience of triumphing over the multiple traumas of my life will bring hope and inspiration to others. In this part of the book I reveal how I accomplished this through three principles and seven pillars and thus became a better person rather than a bitter person.

It is true that the apostle Paul tells us that God's grace is sufficient for any situation in life and that God's power is made perfect in our weakness (2 Corinthians 12:9), but it is *also true* that God expects *us*—as His children—to live wisely and to be willing to do *our* part when dealing with the traumas that come storming completely unexpectedly into our lives. Just as sailors setting out to sea have a plan for dealing with a potential (and likely) storm, so we need to have a plan in place for when we are going to be in the midst of a storm in our life. In the book I describe the plan that (with God's help and wisdom) has enabled me to get through the storms of my life *triumphantly*. Yes, God has promised us that His *"grace is sufficient"* (2 Corinthians 12:9) and that He will give us His wisdom (James 1:5), but that doesn't mean that God is going to work out every problem for us without any effort on our part. As the old adage puts it, "God helps those who help themselves." It also doesn't mean that our Lord Jesus is always going to still the storm (Matthew 8:23–26), but it *does* mean that He will be with us *in the midst of* the storm (Acts 27:23–24). How often in my life I have prayed that God would still the storm—such as healing my beloved wife Marion and my beloved son Kevin and not allowing Alzheimer's to take over my beloved Carolyn's life—but He didn't do any of those things.

However, *all through* those storms and every storm of my life, God has given me His sweet peace and a sense of His glorious presence. I love Annie J. Flint's hymn "God Has Not Promised," which I have sung often through my trials and traumas:

God has not promised skies always blue
Flower-strewn pathways all our lives through.
God has not promised sun without rain
Joy without sorrow, peace without pain…

God has not promised smooth roads and wide,
Swift easy travel, needing no guide;
Never a mountain, rocky and steep
Never a river, turbid and deep

But God has promised strength for the day
Rest for the labor, light for the way
Grace for the trials, help from above
Unfailing kindness, undying love.

Another hymn that has been an inspiration to me during challenging times in my life is "Wonderful Peace," written by Warren D. Cornell (1889), which I hum to myself every night as part of my getting-to-sleep routine:

Far away in the depths of my spirit tonight
Rolls a melody sweeter than psalm.
In celestial-like strains it unceasingly falls
O'er my soul like an infinite calm.

Peace, peace, wonderful peace
Coming down from the Father above!
Sweep over my spirit forever, I pray
In fathomless billows of love!

The book is partly autobiographical and partly a synthesis of my theological and philosophical beliefs with my home-spun theories woven in, and taken together they reveal the person I am. Where we may disagree on any issue, I trust we will do so agreeably.

One day when Pastor Brown was out visiting the flock the Lord said to him, "I want you to drop around and see Mrs. Green today and get matters resolved between you."

"Oh Lord," the pastor responded, "anyone but Mrs. Green."

"No," insisted the Lord, "I want you to visit Mrs. Green."

So the pastor drove around to the house, went up to the door and gently knocked on the door (hoping Mrs. Green wouldn't hear it). "Press the bell," said the Lord. He did, and he heard a movement on the inside. So he knelt down and peered into the keyhole, and there on the other side was Mrs. Green, peering into the same keyhole.

"Oh, Mrs. Green," the pastor blurted out, "finally, after ten years, we are seeing eye to eye."

You, my readers, may not see "eye to eye" with me on every issue I have written about, but it is my prayer that what you read in this book will bring hope and inspiration to your life and the conclusion that God really does care about you.

Our Lord assured us of that when He said to His disciples, and thus to us, "*Look at the birds of the air; they do not sow or reap or store away in barns, and yet your heavenly Father feeds them. Are you not much more valuable than they?*" (Matthew 6:26). Wow! What wonderful assurance of God's love and care for us! No wonder our Lord admonished His disciples to stop worrying about what they were going to eat and drink and wear (Matthew 6:28–32).

As there are (of necessity) some heavy parts in the book, I have endeavoured to keep it (in keeping with my light spirit) as light and smile-inducing as possible.

Anyone who knows me will know that if there is a "silver lining" to be found in any cloud of a trauma, I will gravitate toward that silver lining.

It is my desire that the primary thesis of the book will be not about me but about God's grace, goodness and greatness and for His glory alone, a story of how God has enabled me to be more than triumphant through every vicissitude of my life.

I'm reminded of the many traumatic situations that the apostle Paul experienced in his desire to spread the Good News of the gospel throughout the world. In his letter to his fellow believers at Corinth, he lists 20 of them (2 Corinthians 11:23–28). And yet, in spite of all that he had to go through, he came through *triumphantly*, a living example of what he wrote to his fellow believers at Rome, declaring unto them that "*In all these things we are more than conquerors through him who loved us*" (Romans 8:37), the verse I have used as the theme for this book.

As we go through challenging times in our life, we have choices to make. We can choose to be bitter or better, lugubrious of spirit or light of spirit. We can allow our adversities to break us down or build us up. We can hold "pity parties" or "praise parties." And we can choose to be victims or victors. The choice is ours! I have chosen—through God's grace and strength—the latter of each of these choices. I trust that will be your choice also.

Paul wrote that in all the hardships he had been through in life, he kept in mind that "*We have this treasure [of the gospel] in jars of clay*"—the metaphor he uses for our bodies—"*to show that this all-surpassing power is from God and not from us*" (2 Corinthians 4:7). We too, as followers of our Lord Jesus Christ, can experience this all-surpassing power, whatever traumatic experiences we have to go through in life. Praise be to God!

Finally, this is a very practical, down-to-earth book, written by a very practical, down-to-earth person. My prayer is that it will be an inspiration to all who read it.

## PART ONE

# TRAUMAS REVEALED

# CHAPTER 1

# LOSS OF MY CHOSEN VOCATION

## OUR MARRIAGE

Following my graduation in theology at Toronto Bible College, my first wife and I were married in a beautiful wedding in May 1950. We were both in excellent health at the time, but little did we know that in her early thirties, Marion would be facing a very serious chronic illness that would cause her great physical and emotional suffering. It would also change the course of my vocational life, for which God had gifted me and I had trained.

## MEETING AND COURTSHIP

Marion Slight and I had met at my seventeenth birthday party, which was sponsored by a girl in our church youth group who worked with Marion at General Electric in Toronto, where both of them were secretaries. Marion attended a different church and was a committed Christian, singing in the church choir and teaching a girls' Sunday school class. I too was very involved in my church, teaching a boys' Sunday school class and leading a Friday evening "Happy Hour." It was a program for children ages 5 through 12 that featured Gospel choruses, stories, and Bible-illustrating dramas that I wrote, performed in and directed. As I look back on that period of my life it's hard to believe that I was involved like that while still in my teens, but I already knew that my life work would be in full-time Christian service.

Marion and I had a very happy and activity-filled courtship, even though it was a very difficult time in her life. Her dad had recently been evicted from their home for committing an offence too repulsive to go into here. It's interesting that at the time Marion was dealing with the pain of witnessing her dad being evicted from their home, I too was dealing with a similar painful problem.

Also she had a 30-year-old brother with Down Syndrome, who took up most of her mother's time. She and her other siblings had always felt neglected by their mother, which often happens in families where there is a child who demands almost full-time attention.

However, in spite of all that was going on in her home, Marion was a beautiful fun-loving teenager.

## EARNING MONEY FOR COLLEGE

As I didn't have any money saved up from my many summer jobs to attend college, my parents were not able to help me financially, and there were at that time no government student grants or loans, I needed to work for a year.

I applied for a position I saw advertised for a high school graduate to be assistant to the purchasing agent of a company located in the east end of Toronto that manufactured dry cleaning equipment. I received a phone call to set up an interview. I travelled by streetcar (three different ones) to get to the interview, and when I heard more details about the job (including an attractive salary for a kid just out of high school), I thought, *Wow! I would like this job*.

In a few days I received a phone call from the general manager informing me that I had been accepted for the position and I was to report the following Monday. Wow! What exciting news: my very first full-time job!

On the Monday, I was up bright and early, dressed in the one and only suit I owned, and it was "It's off to work I go," as the seven dwarfs in *Snow White* sang. I received a warm welcome from all the office staff and spent a few days beside the purchasing agent to get my introduction into the world of purchasing. I loved every minute of the job, and after six months I was ecstatic at receiving my first pay increase. Soon I was working on my own, contacting companies by phone to order parts and tools for the factory. I then had to confirm those calls with a typed-out purchase order. What a blessing that I had learned typing skills in high school and in fact was one of the top students in the class!

What I didn't know when I accepted the job was that the company was in the process of building a large new factory and offices in Newmarket. The move to the new location was planned for sometime in early spring. When asked if I would make the move, I didn't hesitate. It would be a great experience for me.

One problem I had was where I would live in the town. No need to worry, as the manager of the painting department, learning that I had decided to go to Newmarket, asked if I would like room and board in his home. He and his wife had just moved into a brand new large house in the town and, as they didn't have any children, thought it would be great to have a young man reside in their home. Once again—as so often in my life—my mom's favourite Bible verse came to mind: "*God will provide*" (Genesis 22:8, NKJV). And He did! The lovely couple (Alf and Ruth) indeed did treat me like a son; in fact they spoiled me with great meals and lots of TLC (tender loving care).

During the time I worked in Newmarket I travelled by bus to Toronto each weekend to spend time with Marion and my family, and we both continued as Sunday school teachers.

## PURCHASING OR PREACHING?

As I was coming to the end of the summer, I had to keep wrestling with the fact that in my heart I knew that God was calling me to full-time Christian service, to be a preacher and pastor. I had to make a decision: Would it be purchasing or preaching? The question had to be settled, and soon! My mom of course had never stopped praying that I would become a preacher. I must confess that the temptation to remain in my present situation was very tempting. I would be able to dress like the purchasing agent (I have always loved nice clothes!), drive a car like he did (I have always loved nice cars!), and live in a nice new house like he did (I had only lived in old rented houses). What to do? I had been taught in my youth that if you have a major decision to make in life, you should spend time in the Word of God and prayer. I dedicated a whole night to doing just that, wrestling with God, and by morning my decision had been made. God and my mom had won out! I would make an appointment with the Toronto Bible College registrar and apply to become a student at the college.

The day after making my decision I made an appointment to meet with the general manager of the company to inform him of my decision to resign from the job and go to Bible college. His response was "Barber college? Why would you leave a position like you have with all its potential to become a barber?" I then said the word "Bible" more clearly and that I was going to train to become a minister. His retort was "That sounds more like something you would go into."

On my last day with the company the staff held a going-away party for me and presented me with a lovely leather briefcase, engraved with my name, which I would use daily at college.

## TRAINING FOR FULL-TIME CHRISTIAN SERVICE

I travelled to Toronto one day to meet with the registrar of the college and apply as a student. In a few days I received a response from him that I had been accepted. Wow! Now I was on my way to becoming what God had been calling me to, a preacher of the Word of God and a pastor to all who would become my parishioners.

Toronto Bible College had been established for the sole purpose of training young men and women for full-time Christian ministry, to serve either as missionaries in a foreign land or in pastoral ministry. I spent wonderful and spiritually enriching years getting deep into the study of God's Word and taking many other related subjects that would prepare me well for my chosen vocation. The curriculum included intense studies of the Bible verse by verse, systematic theology, pastoral psychology, homiletics (art of preparing a sermon), public speaking, Church history, pastoral counselling, psychology, logic (learning about syllogisms), apologetics and more.

During that time, Marion continued in her secretarial job and took evening courses at the same college. We also both continued to teach a Sunday school class in our own churches.

## PAYING MY WAY THROUGH COLLEGE

As my parents were not able to provide any financial support, it was necessary for me to work evenings and summers at part-time jobs, even though I had saved up considerable funds from my job in Newmarket. I also wanted to put away funds for when Marion and I would get married following my graduation.

Having to carry a full student workload and also work part-time didn't leave me much time to date Marion, but as the saying goes, "Love finds a way"—and it did! I felt a little envious of the students whose parents could afford to pay their way, and they could just lounge around in the men's lounge and socialize after school hours. Due to my heavy school load and part-time work load, it became necessary for me to resign from the student council as chair of evangelism. This was a very deep disappointment for me, but as the saying goes, "That's how life goes!"

To save money, I rode my brother's new bike to school every day when the weather was good, even though the streetcar fare was just 25 cents for four tickets. Every so often my dear dad and sister Marjorie would give me money so that I could take the streetcar.

Two part-time evening jobs I had were packing margarine at a factory and assisting the maintenance manager of the college in cleaning the many areas of the college. I packed margarine into cartons as they sped along the conveyor belts. It now reminds me of the scene where Lucy and Ethel on the *I Love Lucy* show were packing chocolates in the chocolate factory, and after their mouths couldn't hold any more, they stuffed them wherever their imaginations led them to. If you remember that one, you will still be able to laugh heartily.

When we were packing the margarine, we had to include one of the colouring packets that were used to change the margarine from white to look more like butter. Farmers insisted that the margarine could not resemble butter. It was such silliness, which of course changed through the years. I worked Monday to Friday evenings from five to nine and made very good money, as it was piecework and I worked very quickly.

During the last two years of my studies, I assisted the maintenance manager in cleaning many areas of the college each day after classes. It was very convenient to have this part-time job without having to travel anywhere. It was a job I enjoyed very much, and it paid quite well. The manager often told me that the school had never looked so clean. I had learned to do housekeeping properly when I was a boy, and it was good training for when I would have to do it so often during my married life. All of my older sisters went out to work in their mid-teens, so we younger ones were assigned many household duties. We washed and dried the dishes and put them in their proper place in the cupboard, mopped or swept the linoleum kitchen floor after every meal, cleaned the toilet (yes, one toilet for 12 people!) and dusted around the house. We seldom ever complained, as we knew it had to be done, my mom was too busy with all her responsibilities, and my older sisters were out to work.

## SUMMER JOBS

In order to earn enough money for the forthcoming school year, I needed to work summer jobs, as well as the after-class jobs I worked at during the school year. I will share two of the most interesting ones.

## SUMMER IN QUEBEC AND SEPARATION FROM MARION

As I approached the end of my first year at Bible college I prayed that God would lead me as to what I should work at for the summer. Then I had a phone call from the superintendent of home missions for our denomination—Dr. John F. Halliday—to ask if I would be interested in serving the Lord for the summer in Quebec at a Christian children's camp. I told him I would pray about it. My first thought naturally was *How will Marion and I deal with being separated for four months and not being able to enjoy activities together?* We prayed about it, and we realized that as soldiers of the Cross it was a small price to pay, particularly when compared to the cost soldiers pay when they go off to war for Canada. Many of them never return to their loves, while others return physically or psychologically wounded for life. My second thought was more practical—*This job will be good training for my vocation.* Some days later I phoned Dr. Halliday back to tell him that I would accept his proposal, and we set up a meeting to discuss details.

Two weeks later I was on my way by train to Montreal. Marion and I had said our sad farewells for the summer, finding it of course very difficult to think of four months of being separated. I also of course said my goodbyes to my family. Mom was in tears, but she assured me she would be praying for me every day.

The founder and director of the camp picked me up at the train station and drove me to the camp, just outside Lachute, which is 62 kilometres west of Montreal. When I found out that the months of May and June would involve long hours of hard physical work, I wondered how I would ever get through it. Log cabins had to be built, and we had to construct a high concrete wall to dam the waters of a pond for a swimming pool. The work on the dam went from early morning to late in the evening, and I can still remember vividly the bites from the swarms of black flies, which left welts on any areas of our skin that were uncovered, and scratching at them all night long. We also had to erect hydro poles to provide electricity for the camp facilities.

## THE BOULDER THAT SAVED MY LIFE

It's actually more correct to say "the boulder that *God used* to save my life." During the erection of one of the 40-foot cedar hydro poles, the man who was supposed to direct the bottom of the pole into the hole lost his footing and the control of the pole. As a result, the pole slipped past the hole, resulting in it crashing groundward. All of the men jumped out of the way—except me. The pole came down on me with its full weight, and had it not been for a boulder that suspended the pole, my neck would have been crushed, and I probably would not have lived to tell this amazing story or to fulfill my vision of becoming a preacher and pastor. God had protected me, as He had plans for my future. Jeremiah, the Old Testament prophet, put it this way to God's people: "*I know the plans I have for you*" (Jeremiah 29:11). That rock has often reminded me of Psalm 18:2: "*The Lord is my rock, my fortress and my deliverer…in whom I take my refuge.*" The rock on the ground in Quebec was certainly the one that provided refuge for me (my neck and my life) that day. Praise be to God!

## ARRIVAL OF CAMPERS

In the first week of July the boys and girls began to arrive for a one- or two-week stay at the camp. These were children from the St. Henri district, a community southwest of Montreal made famous by author Gabrielle Roy's book *The Tin Flute*. Back then it had a mixture of English- and French-speaking families. The children who came to the camp were from the English section of the city, most of them from families that were struggling financially and many of them from dysfunctional homes. Many of them attended the Sunday school of the church that was pastored by the owner of the camp. What a great opportunity to touch these lives with the love of Jesus! My experience of teaching Sunday school classes and directing the children's hour at my local church in years past was a definite advantage.

Throughout the summer, I was a camp counsellor in one of the many log cabins we had built earlier in the summer and was in charge of the after-breakfast devotional time each morning. Of course those who have worked at summer camps will know that you just fill in here and there and do whatever is needed to be done.

As I was very lonely at times, being away from Marion and my family, I was blessed to have wonderful fellowship with the camp staff.

## A DOWNSIDE TO THE SUMMER

The downside of the summer was that the owner of the camp was not able to pay me very much for my summer's work, and it meant that I would have to work longer hours at part-time jobs in the upcoming year at college. Not getting remunerated at the same level as other people with the same skills and training is something you have to get accustomed to in full-time Christian service. It's all part of the price you pay. You had better not be in it for the money!

## LAST DAY AND BACK IN EACH OTHER'S ARMS

On my last day at the camp, the owner drove me to Montreal to board the train for Toronto Union Station, where Marion would meet me and we would once again be in each other's loving arms (and for quite a while too!). We decided that on Saturday we would go to Centre Island for a picnic. That day I met Marion at her home, where she and her mother had prepared a delicious picnic lunch. We took the streetcar to the docks and boarded an island ferry. What a joy to be together again after a long four-month separation! What we didn't know was that the next summer we would be separated again, but at least not so far away from each other.

## SUMMER STUDENT PASTORATE

I was coming to the second year of my theological studies, and I wondered what I should do for the summer. I soon had the answer.

Dr. Halliday, the same man who had phoned me about working at the camp in Quebec, called me again, with the news that a little Baptist church in east Hamilton was looking for someone to be their pastor for the summer, with perhaps a view to calling him as their full-time pastor. The pastor of the church had just resigned, as he had run into some major issues with the board of elders and membership. It didn't sound like the happiest situation to get involved in, but it seemed to me like a great opportunity to get my feet wet (as the saying goes) in what I believed would be my life's work. I had already learned a great deal in my years at Bible college about preaching and pastoring, so I was excited about putting some of it into practice. I agreed to take on the assignment, and within days I had packed my bags and was on the train to go live with a delightful elderly couple for the summer and commence my first pastoral experience.

## MANY FIRSTS

Of course there were many firsts, including observing our Lord's Supper (Communion), baptizing new believers, and officiating at my first wedding ceremony and first funeral service. I didn't experience any anxiety or nervousness before or during any of these firsts, as being in the public eye has always come naturally to me. And further I was leaning on the promise that "*I can do all things through Christ who strengthens me*" (Philippians 4:13, NKJV).

We had a humorous experience at one of our Communion services. The lady who prepared the elements also prepared her son's lunch each morning before he left for work at the steel company. This Sunday she buttered the slices of bread and put in a couple of tomatoes. Unfortunately, she got the bags mixed up, and when I went to break the bread, I had butter all over my fingers. I just went through with the service, and we all had a good laugh about it after. Perhaps Mrs. Bell was trying to butter up her pastor or congregants referred to their pastor after the service as "Butterfingers."

Although being away from Marion for much of the summer wasn't easy for me, she was able to accompany me for a few weekends and stayed at one of the other members' homes. The people loved her pleasant and caring manner and were thinking, I am sure, that she would make a wonderful pastor's wife.

## FALL AND WINTER STUDENT PASTORATE

When I was approaching the end of my summer pastorate in Hamilton, the members decided that they would like me to continue on as the student pastor for the fall and winter while I completed my final year of studies at Bible college. I agreed to do that, and every weekend I travelled by train back and forth between Toronto and Hamilton. It meant that I was a very busy young man with my studies, travels, and work, leaving little time for Marion and me to spend together. She handled it all very well, anticipating—as I was—the day when we would commit ourselves to living together as husband and wife.

During my student pastor days at the church during the summer, fall and winter, many new people attended our services and came into membership. Many of these were parents of children we had reached through our vacation Bible school, our Sunday school, a Friday night children's program, and my work with the youth of the community.

## A CALL TO FULL-TIME PASTORATE

As I was approaching my graduation and the conclusion of my student pastorate, the board and membership decided to extend a call to me to become their full-time pastor. Marion and I prayed about this, and we felt that God would have us accept the invitation and thus launch my full-time pastoral ministry.

## MY GRADUATION

The graduation ceremonies of Toronto Bible College were held in April of each year in Toronto's Varsity Arena on Bloor St. It was always considered a very special event in church circles. In fact it had become known as the religious event of the year in Toronto. TBC (as most people referred to it) graduation ceremonies featured inspiring music from the well-trained college musical groups (mass choir, duets, quartets and solos) and soul-stirring congregational singing by the thousands of people in attendance. Ceremonies at my graduation were no different, except for one thing: I had been chosen to deliver one of the valedictorian addresses. What a thrill! For the first time in my life I would face three thousand people and declare what my years at the college had meant to me and more importantly what God's Word and the Lord Jesus Christ meant to me. What an additional thrill it was to have my mom and nine siblings in the audience praying for me—and probably praying that I wouldn't forget any of my lines! I was just as comfortable in front of thousands as I was in front of the 100 or so in my parish in Hamilton. It was also a joy to have a busload of parishioners from my parish in Hamilton in attendance.

Toronto Bible College was founded in 1894 as an interdenominational training centre for Christian young people who were considering full-time Christian service as a minister or foreign missionary and also for those who simply wanted to further their knowledge of the Bible and related subjects. In 1906 John McNicol became the principal of the school, and he continued in that position until 1946. However, Dr. McNicol continued his lectures until 1954, which meant that I was blessed to sit under his Spirit-filled ministry. He lectured from the series of books he had written, entitled Thinking Through the Bible, taking us students verse by verse through the Word of God. What a joy it was to take in his lectures!

On the occasion of Dr. McNicol's 40th anniversary as principal of TBC, William Lyon Mackenzie King, then prime minister of Canada, wrote, "In our days at the University of Toronto, no undergraduate stood in higher esteem than John McNicol. That regard for his attainments of character and scholarship has grown with the years and today is recognized throughout Canada and the world." No wonder Dr. John McNicol had such a profound influence on my life, both as a student and as a Christian leader, as did all the many professors of the college.

## REACHING YOUTH

When I commenced my student pastorate, the congregation numbered around 30 (mostly older people). However, by the time I completed my three-year full-time pastorate, the attendance had more than quadrupled, with the majority of those being young couples and youth. Reaching youth for Christ has been one of the strongest aspects of my pastoral ministry. I have always believed that if a parish is to have a future ministry, it must reach out to youth in the present. I did so at this parish, my first, by holding gym nights in the local school during the fall and winter, playing softball with youth during the summer, and teaching a youth Bible class on Sunday mornings. What a thrill—in this parish and in all three of my parishes—to look out over the Sunday morning congregation and see so many youth, most of whom I had the joy of bringing into the church and, more importantly, into a personal relationship with the Lord Jesus.

## MY ORDINATION

It was in this church that I was ordained to the Baptist ministry. How lovely that my mom (who had been diagnosed with cancer at that time) could be present for such an important milestone in her son's ministry and hear her son introduced as the Rev. Ernest Nullmeyer. It sounded good to me too!

Marion was very active in the church, leading a monthly women's group, teaching a teenage girls' Sunday school class and visiting the sick and shut-in on her own and also accompanying me. Everyone in the congregation loved her. She was in excellent health at the time and had no idea—thank God—what was ahead in regards to her health.

## MINISTRY TO YOUTH PAID OFF

Many years following my ministry in my first parish, I was preaching at an anniversary service in Toronto, and after the service a tall good-looking young man came up to me and said, "Do you remember me?"

I looked him in the eyes (eyes never change, even though other physical features do) and replied, "I think your first name is Ron."

Well, that brought a big smile to his face, and he responded, "Yes, from Normanhurst Baptist. I came to Christ under your ministry there, and now I am an elder in this church." That brought a huge smile to my face! He then introduced me to his lovely wife and children. Yes, I had through my preaching, teaching, and activities with the youth sown the seed of God's Word, the congregants had watered it with their prayers, and God had brought it to fruition (1 Corinthians 3:5–7). Praise be to God!

## A NEW PASTORATE

As I was approaching the end of three years at my first parish, I received an invitation to preach for a "call" (as Baptists call it) to a little downtown church in Barrie (Collier St. Baptist). The pulpit committee had visited my parish in Hamilton and liked what they heard and saw, particularly impressed, I am sure, with so many youth in the congregation. After hearing me preach, the members voted 100 percent in favour of issuing a call to me, and in March 1953 Marion and I moved to Barrie.

It was not long until the little sanctuary couldn't accommodate the number of people that were attending. It was time to start looking for property outside of the downtown area. We purchased a property, and soon construction began of an edifice that would accommodate our large and growing Sunday services, Sunday school and weekday youth groups. While our new building was under construction we moved our services to a large Independent Order of Foresters (IOOF) hall. Dances were held there on Saturday evenings, so we had to have a large crew of volunteers turn up early on Sunday mornings to clean the place and set up 300 chairs. We then moved to an elementary school around the corner from our new location, which enabled us to use the classrooms for Sunday school classes.

The day we held dedication services in our beautiful new church building was one of the most exciting of my pastoral ministry, and what a joy to have my mom, brother and all eight sisters present for the grand opening!

During my nine-year ministry at what was now called Emmanuel Baptist, I had the joy of seeing the congregation grow exponentially from 40 to over 400. Much of the growth was due to my radio ministry on Wednesday mornings (*Good News Broadcast*) and our Sunday Evening Gospel Hour and maybe a little to my dynamic preaching style and also my appeal to youth. As occurred in my first parish in Hamilton, we witnessed amazing growth in that area of our church life. As I was still in my twenties in my early years at Emmanuel, I had the physical energy and stamina to be involved in all kinds of activities with the youth, including sports. What a joy to have many of our youth go into full-time Christian service and for many to go on serving our Lord in congregations wherever they settled!

While I was the pastor at Emmanuel, we were blessed with three boys coming into our lives: Barry, whom we adopted at six weeks of age, and Kevin and Bradley, sons that Marion gave birth to. Marion was a devoted mother to our three boys, taking an interest in every aspect of their lives and giving them the most important gifts a mother (or father) can give to their children: attention, acceptance, affirmation, appreciation and, above all, affection.

## STORM CLOUDS APPEARING

While I was pastoring at Emmanuel, I began to notice radical changes in Marion's health. She was showing signs of severe lethargy when trying to carry out her responsibilities as a homemaker and a pastor's wife. We made a visit to our family doctor, which became the first of a long series of visits as he tried to diagnose what Marion's health problem was. When he became stymied he sent us to an internist, who also was unable to ascertain the underlying cause of her continuous decline in energy.

Marion also had problems with breathing due to nasal polyps, and she had to go through eight miserable surgeries to remove them. It was yet another health challenge for her to deal with and dragged her down physically and emotionally.

Marion was seen by numerous specialists to try to diagnose her underlying medical problem, and she was prescribed many powerful medications to help lessen the pain she was constantly experiencing in many parts of her body. One drug she was prescribed was prednisone, which can have serious and deleterious side effects, including confusion, anxiety, restlessness, insomnia and mental depression.

When the doctors were unable to come up with a satisfactory diagnosis, one suggested that she must be suffering from neurosis. Only after her medical condition had resulted in constant migraines, the loss of most of her hearing and a kidney and finally liver disease was she diagnosed with an auto-immune disease known as lupus. However, in spite of all her health challenges, she courageously carried on her responsibilities as a loving mother and dedicated pastor's wife.

## MY THIRD AND LAST PASTORATE

The pastor of Stanley Avenue Baptist Church in west Hamilton had recently resigned after a long and successful ministry, so the church was looking for his successor. The pulpit committee had heard of a pastor in Barrie whose ministry had been very much blessed of the Lord. So the committee visited Emmanuel Baptist for a Sunday morning worship service and heard me preach. A point of interest was that the committee arrived late, and because our sanctuary was always filled to capacity, except sometimes the front row, the men (all dressed in dark suits) had to be ushered to the front. That caused my congregants to wonder what might be going on. After the service, the group of seven men asked to meet with me in my study. There they explained that their pastor had resigned and they were looking for a younger man to become the new pastor. I listened with interest, and then the chairman of the committee asked me if I would consider a call to be their new minister. I said I would pray about it, and after we prayed together for God's guidance they left to return to Hamilton.

I had been feeling for some time that perhaps I should be moving on to a new challenge in my ministry. Four weeks after the visit of the pulpit committee, I received a letter from the chair of the committee stating that at a recent meeting of the membership, they had voted 100 percent to have me preach at a Sunday service, with a view to inviting me to be their new pastor. Marion and I prayed about it for a week and concluded that I should accept the invitation to preach at the church, and if they issued a call following that, I would accept.

The membership met and voted 100 percent to invite me to be their new pastor. I commenced my ministry in November of 1962 and saw the blessing of our Lord upon the work for 10 years. During that time we made major renovations to the building (which was 73 years old). These included renovating the washrooms and dividing the lower auditorium into Sunday school departments and a bright new nursery. We also completed the under-construction Christian education wing. During my ministry, the Sunday school tripled from 100 to 300, the youth groups tripled, and Sunday congregations grew, with many new people attending and joining the church.

## MARION'S HOSPITALIZATION

Marion's health continued to decline, so much so that she experienced her second nervous breakdown and a suicide attempt. She was rushed to St. Joseph Hospital, where she was admitted to the psychiatric ward under the care of the director of the ward, Dr. Isaac Sakinofsky. We could not have asked for a more compassionate and competent psychiatrist. These were incredibly painful days for the boys and for me. Here I was with a very ill wife, three boys (ages 16, 13 and 10), and a growing parish. As I look back, I'm amazed that I didn't experience a nervous breakdown. The Bible truths I leaned heavily upon were *"I can do all things through Christ who strengthens me"* (Philippians 4:13, NKJV) and *"My grace is sufficient for you, for my power is made perfect in weakness"* (2 Corinthians 12:9).

Marion was hospitalized for six weeks, and then came the painful transition for her to get back into homemaking and being a pastor's wife. Before she was released from the hospital, the doctor requested that I meet with him. He made it clear that if I didn't change my vocation as a pastor, Marion would be headed toward another nervous breakdown, and even worse. Of course the uppermost thoughts in my mind were *What will I get into?, How does one make the transition from being a pastor to another kind of vocation?* and *Who would want to hire a former pastor?*

I continued on as pastor of the church until I knew what God would lead me into. The elders of the church and the congregants were very understanding through all this challenging time. Once again it was a very painful time for our family. As I look back I thank God for the mature way my boys handled all this adversity in spite of their young age.

## LOSS OF MY CHOSEN VOCATION

The decision I had to make to get out of pastoral ministry (which I loved so much, had been called to and trained for) brought indescribable emotional pain. Indeed it was one the most traumatic experiences of my life! It also caused considerable consternation among my former congregants, who didn't know all the circumstances. Word even got around that "Pastor Nullmeyer had lost his faith." In fact, nothing could be farther from the truth. If ever I needed faith and to lean upon my Lord, it was now! Let me add here that this decision caused Marion very deep guilt feelings about being responsible for me having to leave the ministry. But it was a reality that had to be faced, and I put into practice the three principles that I have written about in part 2, chapter 1: accept, adapt, and advance. And more importantly, I leaned heavily on the promises of God as the prophet Isaiah articulates them: "*Don't you be afraid, for I am with you. Don't be dismayed, for I am your God. I will strengthen you…I will help you…I will uphold you with the right hand of my righteousness*" (Isaiah 41:10, WEB) and "*I, the LORD, have called you in righteousness; I will take hold of your hand*" (Isaiah 42:6). The Psalmist declares, "*You hold me by my right hand*" (Psalm 73:23).

How often we see children who panic about something, and as soon as a parent takes hold of their hand, they settle down and look up and smile at Mommy or Daddy. They know that they are in good hands. That's how we should feel, knowing that we are in God's hands at all times! "*Don't be afraid… When you pass through the waters, I will be with you*" (Isaiah 43:1–2, WEB). That deserves a "Wow!"

## NOW WHAT?

Now the question became, what should I do for employment? Who wants to hire a former Baptist minister? I decided to lean heavily on a Bible passage I had memorized in my youth: "*Trust in the LORD with all your heart, and lean not on your own understanding; In all your ways acknowledge Him [bring God into the circle and centre of your problem], and He shall direct your paths*" (Proverbs 3:5–6, NKJV). Another passage became a light in the dark tunnel of uncertainty for me: "*Do not be anxious about anything, but in every situation, by prayer and petition, with thanksgiving, present your requests to God. And the peace of God, which transcends all understanding, will guard your hearts and your minds in Christ Jesus*" (Philippians 4:6–7). That deserves another "Wow!"

## AMAZING PHONE CALL

While I was out of work, God was at work! He always is in His children's lives. He is our Heavenly Father, and He will never leave us or forsake us. The Psalmist writes, "*As a father has compassion on his children, so the LORD has compassion on those who fear him*" (Psalm 103:13). And here's how I paraphrase verse 14: "Our Heavenly Father knows all about us; He remembers how fragile we can be, just like dust." My Heavenly Father knew how weak and helpless I was feeling, as a husband and a father.

Yes, God *was* at work, so it didn't take long for my prayer for employment to be answered. Another Bible verse came to mind: "*Before they call I will answer*" (Isaiah 65:24).

Some weeks after my meeting with the doctor—and with the employment aspect of my life in limbo—a former member of my parish in Barrie called me. He had had lunch with a friend of his, who was also a former member of my Barrie parish and a board member of Canadian Keswick Bible Conference, and they were looking for a new conference director. He said that he didn't know why but my name had come to his mind. Of course *I* knew why! He then asked me if I would be interested in meeting to discuss the matter. Without hesitating I said, "Yes, I would be interested."

A meeting was set up with the executive of the board of directors. I met with them in Toronto, and after considerable questioning they offered me the position. Once again I didn't hesitate, as this would relieve Marion of her responsibilities of being a pastor's wife, give me the opportunity to still be involved in Christian service, and of course make it possible for me to continue to provide the necessities of life for my wife and sons.

Keswick—as it was affectionately called by the thousands of Canadians and Americans who had been there as guests through the years—was the largest and most prestigious Christian summer resort in North America. I commenced my new type of Christian ministry in April 1972. I write about other Keswick details in part 1, chapter 2.

# CHAPTER 2
# LOSS OF EMPLOYMENT

It has been said that when your employment is terminated, there's not only a financial matter to be concerned about but emotional pain that results from not knowing what to do next, especially if you still have a dependent family to support.

That is the situation I found myself in when I was informed that Canadian Keswick Conference could no longer afford my salary, and being the highest-paid employee I was first to be given my termination notice. When I was hired as the conference director, as I have mentioned in chapter 1, there was a fly in the ointment that I was not informed about but should have been.

First some details about Keswick, as it was popularly known. It was a large and very successful Christian retreat and resort in beautiful Muskoka, where thousands of Christians from Canada and the United States would gather together during the summer months for a vacation in a Christian atmosphere. The program featured well-known Bible teachers from around the world and the very best in Christian music. The chapel, which could accommodate over one thousand, was always filled to capacity on Sundays and weeknights. It also became well-known for many other reasons, including its magnificent gardens, the very best in cuisine served in the 400-seat dining room overlooking beautiful Lake Rosseau, and an action-filled recreation program.

In the late 1960s, three factors played out that eventually put this amazing Christian conference into bankruptcy and me out of employment. At a time when interest rates were rising exponentially, the conference was hit with huge unplanned costs relating to the following:

1. Directives of the Muskoka Region Health Department to upgrade the sewage system.
2. Directives of the Office of the Fire Marshall to upgrade the safety systems.

3. Conference board of directors' decision to proceed with the building of the youth camp on property across from the conference without first having all the funds in place. They didn't take our Lord's admonition seriously when He said, "*Suppose one of you wants to build a tower. Won't you first sit down and estimate the cost to see if you have enough money to complete it?*" (Luke 14:28).

During the centennial year the federal government was dispensing millions of dollars in grants to organizations that were involved in reaching out to inner-city youth. The board of directors applied for a grant for the camp, and they were so sure they would receive one that they proceeded with construction. Keswick Youth Camp was to be no tent or cabin operation but first class in every way. The program included the teaching of canoeing, sailing and even horseback riding. The purpose of the camp was to reach unchurched youth of well-to-do-families with the Christian message, a noble concept to be sure.

Partway through construction the board of directors learned that their application for a government grant had been turned down, as the rates that were going to be charged were out of reach for the families of inner-city youth and would only be appropriate for youth from well-to-do families. What to do now? The board had to apply to the bank for a huge mortgage, placed on the equity of Keswick Conference. The bank granted it but in hindsight probably wished it hadn't. A bank is always reluctant to declare bankruptcy in the case of a religious organization, which is why they seldom get involved in a mortgage on a facility to be used for religious purposes.

Construction on the youth camp was completed, and it operated very successfully for a number of years under the very capable leadership of John Wilkinson; but when the conference was not able to keep up with even the interest payments, the bank moved in and put the conference and the youth camp into bankruptcy. As I was the highest-paid employee, I was the first to be let go.

So here I was with a family to support with no income and no equity to fall back on. Once again my mom's oft-repeated Bible promise brought peace of mind ("God will provide"), and we would bank on that! We did, and I would soon have employment again, which is an amazing story that follows in chapter 3.

## KESWICK IN HINDSIGHT

In hindsight the Keswick experience brought great blessing to our family.

1. It enabled Marion to be free of the duties and responsibilities imposed on her as a pastor's wife. Being the gregarious person she was, she enjoyed socializing with the guests, and they in turn enjoyed socializing with her. She was a great asset to my ministry at Keswick, as she was in my pastorates!
2. As a family, it gave us the opportunity to spend the summers together in beautiful Muskoka and to enjoy all the amenities of the conference, including gourmet meals in the elegant dining room.
3. It provided summer employment for our sons and the opportunity to have fellowship and fun with over 75 youth who were members of my staff.
4. It gave me an opportunity to continue—although in a little different way—my pastoral ministry. I became the summertime pastor to the youth on my staff, and that was a delightful experience. Early every morning I met with the staff and shared a thought with them from God's Word and prayed with them that God would make each one of them a blessing to the guests. I have always loved working with youth, and through the years God has been pleased to bless my ministry among them.
5. I was able to continue my preaching ministry. Every morning after breakfast the guests would gather in what was known as Delectable Mansion and I would lead a 15-minute devotional time. Many guests said that they received as much spiritual blessing from those few minutes as they did at the hour-long chapel services with well-known preachers from around the world.

There are many times when our lives take twists and turns that we find challenging to face, but when we face them knowing that "*I can do all things through Christ who strengthens me*" (Philippians 4:13, NKJV) and that "*My God will meet all your needs according to the riches of his glory in Christ Jesus*" (Philippians 4:19), we can then look back and thank God for what seemed at the time to be an exasperating detour.

It has been said that when one door closes, God will open another door. That door was about to open! Praise be to God!

# CHAPTER 3

# LOSS OF EMPLOYMENT AGAIN

When my employment at Keswick Conference was terminated, I needed to pray for God's guidance as to my next step. In my youth I learned a biblical proverb that says, "*In all your ways acknowledge Him, And He shall direct your paths*" (Proverbs 3:6, NKJV). The apostle James writes, "*If any of you lacks wisdom, you should ask God, who gives generously to all without finding fault, and it will be given to you*" (James 1:5). I have banked on those promises throughout my life, and once again I needed to put the principle into practice. As I walked the streets of Barrie and along the shoreline of beautiful Kempenfelt Bay (walking is good for us physically and therapeutic emotionally), pondering what my next step (pardon the pun) should be, I felt only a sense of peace, knowing that God was in control and something would turn up in His time. It was a difficult time of uncertainty for Marion—as her health was continuing to decline—and for our boys, who were still in school.

## LIGHT IN THE TUNNEL

One evening while Marion and I were reading and the boys were out and about, the phone rang. It was Vic Jackson, a member of my former parish of Emmanuel Baptist. Vic was brought up in a little village outside of Barrie and attended a one-room schoolhouse. Unfortunately, he—like the NHL (National Hockey League) coach Jacques Demers and many Canadians—had slipped through the school system and graduated illiterate. However, like Demers, who later became a Canadian senator, Vic didn't allow this problem to control his life. When he graduated from grade 8 at age 15, he got a job working with a carpenter who took a keen interest in him and noticed that he was a natural when it came to handling tools and operating machines. After a number of years apprenticing, Vic decided it was time to launch out on his own, and he established the Vic

Jackson Renovation Company. The business was very successful, and he learned how to work around his illiteracy problem, as so many people with the same challenge do.

On the phone, Vic expressed his regrets that I had been let go at Keswick and wondered if I would like to do some work for him. In my inimitable manner, I responded, "Sure; what do you have in mind?"

"Well," he said, rather hesitatingly, "it's digging postholes and installing a fence around the property of…" and he mentioned the man's name. This man was a very successful and wealthy businessman. He and his wife lived in a multi-million dollar mansion on the shores of Kempenfelt Bay. They were not members of my parish but would often attend our Sunday evening services, along with many people from other churches that had only morning services. When I met Vic at the job site, of course the owners were rather shocked to see the Rev. Ernest Nullmeyer in work clothes. Vic showed me what to do, and I started in to dig the postholes and erect this mammoth fence. It took me four weeks, and at the end the owners thanked me for doing such a great job. Little did I (or the owners) know that sometime in the future, I would be back at their home decorating it, having established Nullmeyer Decorating. It's a good lesson for my beloved grandchildren and all youth to remember: Always do your best, because you never know what it will lead to.

## NOW WHAT?

The question of course on my mind—and on the minds of my beloved family—was "What will I do next to keep money coming into our home?" There was no need to worry, as Vic (and God) had it all planned out. Vic thanked me for the excellent job I had done erecting the fence and then said he would be in touch with me if something turned up. I didn't have to wait long!

Vic had been awarded the contract to install all the door and window hardware in Barrie's new Riverwood subdivision. One day the superintendent asked him if he knew someone who would do an excellent job on paint touch-ups in the homes that had recently had their one-year inspections. The person for the job had to be very trustworthy, as most of the owners would be out to work. Vic said, "I know the very man for the job; he is as honest a man as you could ever meet." Vic contacted me to see if I was interested in this six-week contract.

My answer? "Yes, indeed!" I went to meet the superintendent, and he hired me within minutes. The following Monday I commenced this job, which was so right for me as it was relaxing and therapeutic, and it provided six weeks of income. And amazingly it was a harbinger of what would eventually become my new vocation—painting and decorating.

One of the homes was owned by a young medical doctor who had recently moved to Barrie to set up her family practice. When I had finished the job, she thanked me for my excellent work. Once again, little did I know that someday in the future that excellent work would lead to a large contract for redecorating her whole house from a contractor's beige to a beautiful colour scheme that I would draw up for her. Yes, we never know when we are planting a seed that will take root and bloom in the future.

## WHAT'S NEXT?

So with that job completed, what would be next? Another phone call from Vic, asking me if I would be interested in working with him on a big renovation job. He said, "Before you answer, let me describe the job." It was going to start out as a very dirty job, as all the plaster and lath had to be removed from the ceilings and walls and then replaced with drywall.

He continued, "You will have to wear old clothes, and we will be wearing masks." Well, the mask aspect wouldn't be new to me, as I had donned masks many times when making pastoral calls on parishioners in hospital isolation wards. Oh, the ironies of life, going from one mask to another!

He paused then for my answer, and as always I said, "Sure, I'll work with you on that job." He would meet me at the house on Monday morning and introduce me to the owners, who would then be on their way to their offices of a company they owned and operated. I would eventually work for that company. Really? Yes, really! That's an amazing and wonderful part of the story that will come to light shortly.

On Monday morning, I was up bright and early (as I am always am), ate breakfast with Marion and the boys, packed a lunch and went off to work, no doubt singing praises to God for opening up this new employment opportunity. And sing all day long I did, even right through the mask shielding my lungs from the fine plaster dust. Eventually we got all of the plaster and lath removed and installed the drywall, and the ceilings and walls were now ready for painting.

## ALWAYS DOING OUR BEST

As Vic had warned me, it was indeed a dirty job, but one that paid off. Indeed, we never know how one job well done will lead to something even better. Let me insert here a wonderful proof of that statement. It comes from the Bible story of Abraham sending his chief servant out, along with ten of his camels and *"all kinds of good things,"* to find a wife among his own people for his son Isaac (Genesis 24). I have taken the liberty to give you the Ernie Nullmeyer translation of the story, just as I would tell it—extemporaneously—if I were relating it in the pulpit.

## THE JOB THAT PAID OFF HANDSOMELY

The servant and his entourage of camels made their way to a little town where Abraham's brother Nahor lived. On arrival in the town, the servant had the camels kneel down near the town well. He then prayed, "O Lord, God of my master, give me success today, and show kindness to my master Abraham. Today at sunset, when the town's daughters come out to the well to draw water, direct me to the one whom I should take back to my master for his son Isaac. I will know that one because when I ask her for a drink, she will give me one and then will offer to give water to all the camels as well."

Before he had finished praying (God often answers our prayers even before we complete them), Rebekah came out with her jar on her shoulder. She was stunningly beautiful and a virgin. While she was filling her jar with water, the servant ran to meet her and said, "Could you please give me a drink of water from your jar?" She quickly lowered the jar to her hands and gave him a drink.

When he was finished drinking, Rebekah made an astonishing offer: "I'll draw water for your camels too, until they're all filled up." (Watering camels is no small task, as a camel's holding tank is about 114 litres, or 30 gallons, and it takes about 13 minutes to get the task done. That's just one camel; Rebekah had ten to fill up. But her faithfulness in carrying out that task was wonderfully rewarded!) After spending the night in the home of Rebekah, the servant returned home with her and his entourage, praising God that he had been led to the right person to be Isaac's wife.

Yes, a job well done will always reap rewards eventually. The dirty job I had accepted and worked at with all my might was to lead to an office job beyond my fondest imagination. One day, while we were having a snack break, the owner of the house returned from his office to see how we were getting along. After a few minutes, he drew me aside and asked me if we could have coffee together sometime. I had no idea why he was inviting me to have coffee with him, but I told him I would be happy to do that. He related the time and place we would meet. When he left, I asked Vic why this gentleman would want to have coffee with me. With a little grin on his face he said, "I think you'll be glad you met with him, but that's all I can share with you right now." Vic was in on the plan. And of course God was at work in my life, as He always has been. The fulfillment of the promise of Psalm 23:1 was at hand: "*The LORD is my shepherd; I shall not want*" (NKJV).

## THE MEETING

We met and ordered and sipped coffee, and his first sentence was "Well, Ernie, you must be wondering why I wanted to get together with you."

I responded, "For sure! And so are my wife and sons."

"Well," he continued, "Vic has shared with me a little about your past, and as I have watched you work and listened to you express yourself, the idea came to me that you just might fit into a new position I am opening up in my company." He then elucidated what the company was all about and what the job description would look like.

The more he talked, the more I was getting a warm feeling that this was a position I would indeed fit into and love. I would become the general manager of the aluminum company. When he said what the starting salary would be, plus the provision of a new car, I said under my breath, "Thank You, Lord. This sounds just like what I need in my life right now." After I recovered from being a little in shock, I responded with "I would love to accept your offer." We shook hands on the deal (no signing of any document) and agreed that I would commence my new job the following Monday.

Vic's response? Sheer delight! Marion's and the boys' response? Absolute delight! Remember one of my mom's favourite Bible verses? "*God will provide*" (Genesis 22:8, NKJV). And for four years and three months I enjoyed every aspect of the job, even getting into sales, which, because I was well-known in the Barrie area, became a little gold mine for me—and my family.

When employees of the company found out that I was an ordained minister, "Pastor Ernie" became my new appellation. This led to many interesting discussions and even counselling sessions, which I did freely and free of charge. One of the salesmen was having a rough time in his marriage, and I was able to help him work through it. Yes, once a pastor, always a pastor! One of the spin-off benefits of my job was that I could provide part-time work for my sons after school, Saturdays, and summers.

## BAD NEWS!

The company continued to expand, but it began to get into deep financial cash flow problems, through purchasing new trucks as well as erecting a new headquarters. As a result, the bank became concerned and declared the company bankrupt. As I was one of the highest-paid employees, I was first to receive my termination letter. However, I didn't panic, as I knew that the Good Shepherd of Psalm 23:1 would provide for me and my family in another way. It was of course a rather troubling time for Carolyn, who had now become my wife and the boys' stepmother. Once again I was without employment and income. *So… what do I do now?* Back to prayer: "Lord, where do I go from here?" And back to leaning on my mom's favourite Bible verse: "*God will provide*" (Genesis 22:8, NKJV).

### GOOD NEWS!

And here is where the sun began to shine again (as it always does!) as you will read in the following pages.

### BANKRUPTICIES AND TERMINATIONS BEGONE!

The evening after my termination from the aluminum company, I gathered Carolyn and the boys around our kitchen table and told them the bad news. There was no sense of panic expressed, but we all agreed that for the time being we would have to tighten our belts, and this included cancelling a trip to Cuba that Carolyn and I had planned for our first wedding anniversary. We all held hands while I prayed for God's guidance and peace, and we left the table knowing that "this too will pass" (one of Carolyn's favourite sayings when something went wrong).

### A VISION IN THE NIGHT

That night I had difficulty sleeping, which is unusual for me, whatever the circumstances of life might be. It wasn't a feeling of anxiety that was keeping me awake and alert; it was a feeling of excitement and anticipation.

There's an old facetious saying, "When all else fails, pray." That has never been the modus operandi of my life, as I resort to prayer immediately when something goes awry. After all, no matter how distressing or vexing the matter might be, God has the solution all worked out. All we have to do is "*wait on the* LORD" (Psalm 27:14, NKJV)—which is not always easy—and He will reveal His will to us.

The same thoughts came bouncing around in my mind: *Ernest, maybe it's time to launch your own business, and then you will never get terminated, and you'll be your own boss.* The thought came back to me that I had heard many years before: *If someone turns a hobby into a business they will have life made.* I went over the things that I was proficient at and enjoyed, and I kept coming back to one: decorating. *Yes, that's it; I will establish my own decorating business!* I felt like waking up Carolyn to tell her my plans for my new job, but as she always (unlike me) had difficulty getting back to sleep, I would wait until the morning. Soon I was going through my Bible verse and hymn routine, and I fell into a deep and peaceful sleep.

## MORNING FOLLOW-UP

When I awoke early the next morning (I'm a morning person), I could hardly wait until Carolyn awoke to reveal my revelation. And when she did wake up and I said that I had something really exciting to share with her, she responded with "Could we just wait until after breakfast?" So we did—as I had no choice.

I began to tell her about the new venture I believed God was leading me into. Her first reaction was her usual one: "Uh, huh." Then her keen mind went into motion. First question—and an insightful one: "What would you do for a vehicle?" And then, "What would you do about equipment?" And "How are you going to get customers?" And "What would you call it?"

Well, I had those all worked out in my mind, and told her.

For a vehicle I would start out just using my little Mazda coupe. As to how I would cram all the supplies and equipment into that little space—I would just make it work!

For equipment and supplies, I would simply go to the appropriate stores and purchase them.

To get customers, I would place an ad in the local newspaper. And here is where the name of the company becomes relevant. As I was well-known in the area (having pastored Emmanuel Baptist Church for nine years, during which time I produced two weekly Christian radio broadcasts), I would call it Nullmeyer Decorating. I drew up an ad and took it to the *Barrie Examiner*, and my new business was launched.

## FIRST CONTRACT

Within two days I had a call from a lady who operated a hair salon in downtown Barrie. She had for years coiffed Carolyn's hair, as well as her mom's and two sisters'. She said she would like her big old house completely redecorated. Wow! Sounded like an amazing first contract. As Carolyn had not yet gotten back into teaching, she volunteered to help me. If she had known what stage one was, she may not have volunteered; but on the other hand, being a farm girl she was no stranger to hard and not-so-pleasant jobs.

## OFF AND RUNNING

We loaded up my little Mazda and were off to our first contract. When we arrived, Hyacinth was a little shocked to see Carolyn Cameron (as she had known her) at her door and even more shocked that the man she had talked to on the phone was really the Reverend Ernest Nullmeyer, whom she had heard preach every Sunday evening and Wednesday morning on the local radio station.

After she got over her shock, she walked us through the century-old house to show us what she wanted done. She didn't even ask for a quote, as she had decided that she wanted my company (my wife and me at that time) to do the job. It was a big contract and would even require me to hire my first employees. Yes, things were taking off fast, even faster than I could have envisioned—even being the visionary I am!

The wallpaper looked like it came from the first batch ever printed. Seniors will remember those old embossed wallpapers. So we started in, removing wallpaper, and at bedtime could feel every muscle in our bodies. It was arduous physical work, and I understood why Carolyn was only able to take a few days of it, but I will say that, just like a girl brought up on the farm who knew how to do chores, she gave it her very best.

## CAROLYN'S NEW POSITION

I still had an important position in my company for Carolyn, and that was answering the phone. Often when I was out doing estimates the client would ask, "Who is that lady who answers your phone with that warm, friendly voice?" I was always proud to respond, "That's my wife."

I have always been amazed that some businesses, organizations and professional offices hire people to answer their phones who do not have a warm, friendly voice. They answer as if you are interrupting them from doing something important. That's not the tone of voice they heard when they phoned Nullmeyer Decorating.

## NEWSPAPER AD PAY-OFF

Soon—as a result of my little ad in the local paper—the phone calls for estimates began to pour in. The timing for the launch of my new business was perfect, as people were beginning to think of spring cleaning and, of course, along with that, spring decorating. Yes, the old saying is true: "Timing is everything!" Plus, home owners would also be thinking about exterior painting. That would give me the opportunity to hire students for the summer and a manager to oversee my offspring company I named Keen and Kleen Student Painters. My son Kevin—who was now a university student—managed that part of the business and even hired his younger brother Brad to work for him. Brad always said (jokingly) that if there was painting to be done in a difficult spot Kevin would assign that to him. That was Kevin—the prankster.

The student painting company did very well, with one of the spin-offs being that the students, who became very efficient painters, would then be moved along to work with me. Two of these were lovely young female high school students that Kevin had hired. Trust Kevin to hire lovely ladies. Eventually—with my training—they developed excellent skills in wallpapering as well as in painting. Michelle and Aleke had emigrated from Holland with their parents and four siblings. They—and eventually three of their sisters, who also worked with me—were all amazing workers. They never needed to be prodded to work harder and didn't require repeated instructions about the jobs they were assigned.

One summer I signed a very large contract for painting the entire offices and factory of a big company in Barrie. The problem was, I had lined up a week-long preaching engagement at a family camp in Muskoka. What should I do? I made the decision to leave the Dutch sisters in charge. When I returned, the president told me that they had the crews working harder than I had them working when I was in charge. Wow! What a blessing to have staff of that calibre.

All my staff was of high calibre. I paid them well, and when we made big money on a contract I shared it with them through bonuses. I have always believed that a company is only as good as its employees. Notice I do not speak of my employees as working *for* me but rather *with* me. We worked as a team or, as a certain department store calls their employees, associates.

It is any wonder that my company—my very own company, Nullmeyer Decorating—was off and running (or would that be painting, wallpapering and designing?), and it became one of the highest respected and largest decorating companies in Simcoe County. Yes, God was with me as my partner.

## CHAPTER 4
# LOSS OF MY BELOVED FIRST WIFE

I have written in chapter 1 about Marion's many years of suffering from a chronic illness, which was eventually—after many years—diagnosed as lupus. She was an amazingly courageous person. As I look back on the way she carried on her responsibilities as a faithful wife, a loving mother and a devoted servant of Christ, it leaves me with a deeper appreciation of the strong and beautiful person she was.

Because of Marion's never-ending migraine headaches and other constant physical pains—resulting, as I have related, in nervous breakdowns—we did have incredibly tough and distressing times as a family. We also had countless numbers of good times together. We had lots of fun around our home and enjoyed lots of picnics, which Marion loved to the full, and several trailer trips in many parts of Canada. We also enjoyed a couple of vacations in Florida during the March break. In spite of always feeling below par, she didn't lose her light spirit and sense of humour. As a family we laughed often together.

In public, she never disclosed how ill she actually felt. She was a born minister, always desiring to minister to the needs of others. After the completion of her earthly journey, many people told me how Marion had ministered to them in their times of need. She loved writing encouraging notes to people who needed an emotional or spiritual lift. She never wallowed in self-pity.

## WHY NOT ME?

However, through the many days, weeks, months and years of just not feeling well, she would ask, "If God seems to be healing other people, why not me?" It was a valid question when so many Christians who claimed to have received a miraculous physical healing were not involved, as she was, in full-time Christian service. She would ask, "Why would God heal an eighty-year-old lady of cancer and not heal me, still in my forties, with so much to live for?" And, I might add, so many people to bless with her loving, caring spirit. The "whys" could go on ad infinitum. The answer is, we don't know why.

## ANOINTING WITH OIL

Through the years of my pastoral ministry, many Christians, knowing of Marion's long struggle with illness, would ask me if she had ever been anointed with oil and prayed over by the elders of the church. This question of course emanates from a passage in the Bible: "*Is anyone among you sick? Let them call the elders of the church to pray over them and anoint them with oil in the name of the Lord. And the prayer offered in faith will make the sick person well; the Lord will raise them up*" (James 5:14–15). The answer to the question is yes. Marion was anointed with oil on several occasions by spiritual men of God in a number of denominations (even Pentecostal, as her mom insisted on), but she was not—*was not*—healed physically. How much of the physical and emotional stress that Marion suffered for 17 years could have been obviated and how much distress my beloved sons and I could have been saved from if Marion had been healed of her disease! How wonderful if she had been healed so that I could have remained in my called-of-God vocation! But she wasn't healed! And then the question why, which she asked almost daily for all those years. My answer to the question is simply "I do not know." And neither does anyone else, except God. As the apostle Paul tells us, when he had prayed—three times even—that God would remove the "*thorn in my flesh*," God's answer was "*My grace is sufficient for you*" (2 Corinthians 12:7–9).

## PHYSICAL HEALING: ACT OF GOD OR ACT OF NATURE?

It does seem that some people experience physical healing that amazes even the doctors. Does this mean that they're acts of God or just unusual acts of nature? I don't know. I do know, though, that the majority of these so-called miraculous healings involve cancer. Why? I don't know. I do know that I have never heard of these healings involving Alzheimer's disease. If cancer, why not Alzheimer's? I don't know. I find peace just leaving all these matters in the hands of my all-wise and loving Heavenly Father.

## CLAIMS TO MIRACULOUS PHYSICAL HEALING

When I put on my skeptic's hat I have often wondered, if the so-called faith healers have the power to bring healing to people when they pray over them, wouldn't it make more sense for them to visit one of the many children's hospitals in North America and pray for and witness the healing of thousands of precious children suffering from cancer and a host of other diseases? I once asked a so-called faith healer that question, and he walked away from me with a smirk on his face.

## SHOULD WE PRAY FOR HEALING FOR OTHERS?

I have been often asked whether or not I pray for people to be healed physically. My answer is simply no. But I do pray that they will sense the presence and peace of God and experience His grace through their trial. That to me is what is most important when dealing with matters beyond our control.

Of course even all those who were healed in the Bible eventually died, as we are all destined to do (Hebrews 9:27). What is most important is that we have experienced spiritual healing through the finished work of Jesus on the Cross, that we are experiencing the glorious grace and peace of our Lord and Saviour, whatever life and nature may throw at us, and that we live in anticipation of that great day when our Lord will *transform our lowly bodies so that they will be like his glorious body*" (Philippians 3:21). Hallelujah!

For a more complete coverage of the subject of physical healing see appendix 1, "Bad Things and God's Will."

## FINAL DAYS

As Marion approached her late forties her health declined exponentially. Our family spent a week in Florida, and she slept the whole week, getting up only to go out for meals. She also slept the whole way home on the plane. As soon as we arrived back in Barrie, I took her to the emergency department in the hospital, and she was admitted immediately. She was diagnosed with a serious liver infection, and after six weeks of being bedridden, she completed her earthly journey and commenced her eternal journey on March 2, 1976, one day after our dear son Brad's 16th birthday.

My sons and I realized afresh that life is certainly not simple, smooth or stationary. It was an incredibly sad time for us all, but the support we gave one another was a beautiful thing. And the support my sons gave their dad was everything any father could ask for! And so, with a strong and vibrant faith, we journeyed on together. We accepted, adapted and advanced.

I am sure that Marion heard the voice of her Lord—whom she loved and served so well—saying unto her, "*Well done, thou good and faithful servant... enter though into the joy of thy lord*" (Matthew 25:21, KJV). Indeed, she was now "safe in the arms of Jesus" with no more pain and no more struggling!

Like the apostle Paul coming to the end of his earthly journey, Marion could say,

> *The time for my departure is near. I have fought the good fight, I have finished the race, I have kept the faith. Now there is in store for me the crown of righteousness, which the Lord, the righteous Judge, will award to me on that day—and not only to me, but also to all who have longed for his appearing.* (2 Timothy 4:6–8)

Amen and amen!

## A TRIBUTE TO OUR FAMILY PHYSICIANS

During her 17 years of dealing with lupus disease, Marion was seen by numerous doctors. Three who were of special help to her, especially in an emotional way, were Dr. John Postnikoff and Dr. Rick Irvin of Barrie and psychiatrist Dr. Isaac Sakinofsky, then director of psychiatry at Hamilton Medical Centre.

# CHAPTER 5
# LOSS OF MY BELOVED SON

Carolyn and I were just finishing breakfast the morning of March 10, 2010, when our conversation was interrupted by the ringing of the phone. On the other end of the line was our daughter-in-law Vicki. I could sense from the tone of her voice that she had something very serious to relate to me. Indeed she did, as she said that our son Kevin had been admitted to Toronto's Sunnybrook Hospital two days previous, and the doctors said the family should be notified, as they were not sure they could pull him through. If ever I went into shock it was at that moment! I assured her that we would start on our way down immediately.

When we arrived at the hospital we were ushered to the isolation ward to put on the appropriate garments in order to visit Kevin. When we walked in, I went into deeper shock. There was my beloved son, whom I had talked to (and punned with, as was our custom) just a few days before, now in a comatose state and on life-support equipment literally from the top of his head to the soles of his feet. I broke into convulsive weeping as, even though I had faced many painful situations in my life, nothing came close to this one! I will ever be grateful to God for one of his nurses, who—contrary to medical practice—put her arms around me and held me tight to try to quiet me down, and of course to my beloved wife Carolyn, who had already wrapped her arms around me. When I finally settled down, the staff requested that I leave the room so that they could do what had to be done. As I walked out into the hall, I saw a group of the medical staff talking about Kevin's case and what to do. I introduced myself to the head doctor and tried to concentrate on what she was conveying to me. Kevin had an immune-system-destroying and life-threatening virus (hemophagocytosis), so rare that they had to send a sample to an American lab for diagnosis.

During the next five months Kevin was in and out of consciousness and, in fact—through very expensive and powerful medications—appeared to be beating the condition. Carolyn and I remember so well the day we visited him and he was sitting up in bed and in his inimitable style (that is, with much enthusiasm) said, "Let's go down to the cafeteria for lunch." We got a wheelchair for him and pushed him down to the cafeteria, where he ate a good lunch and joked and laughed with us, as only Kevin could do. What a beautiful memory God gave us that day to hang on to forever, as we would certainly need it!

At this time in his journey, Kevin's condition seemed to be improving. It looked like the powerful and very costly drugs were working, so much so that they moved him from isolation into a general ward. There, no doubt because of his very low resistance, he came down with C. difficile, which was too much for his system to handle. On August 9, 2010 (five months into his illness), he completed his earthly journey and commenced his eternal journey.

Could Kevin have beaten the virus if he had sought medical advice earlier or if he had been kept in the isolation ward longer? We will never know the answer to those questions.

Here's what we do know though:

1. Kevin could not have had better medical attention than he received. All the doctors and nurses were just so dedicated to getting him better. They were also helpful to all of us family members, who were going through very deep emotional pain.
2. Kevin could not have received more loving family attention than he did from his beloved wife, Vicki, his two boys, Brook and Taylor (both in their teens), and his brothers and their wives and children.
3. Even though Kevin's earthly journey lasted only 52 years, he had lived his life to the full.

## A TRIBUTE TO MY BELOVED SON

Kevin (like his mom) had a creative flair for decorating. While growing up, he would decorate his bedroom door in keeping with the season of the year. They were quite the works of art.

From his earliest years his mother and I knew we had a son who was not going to let any grass grow under his feet. Kevin was a fast learner, which was evidenced in how early in life he learned to walk and talk. When he was just a little gaffer he would come to my workshop to see what I was building and ask if he could help me with it. It's no wonder that he became quite the master craftsman, even designing and building beautiful furniture for his home and summer residence. He would tackle anything and everything, believing (like his dad) that if someone else could do it, so could he.

He was an excellent student and all through elementary and secondary school was known as the life of the class. Like his dad he wanted to get as much fun out of life as possible, whatever he was involved in, and you would not be with Kevin very long before your spirits were lifted.

## BACKGROUND

Kevin also loved music and did well on the euphonium, which he first learned to play (sort of) at a summer music school in Hamilton. It was rather painful at times for the family to listen to him practice, but we got through it. He eventually played euphonium in the award-winning Barrie Central Collegiate band, which he travelled with for performances in France. Carolyn played the sax and back in the sixties had also been a member of that well-known band and travelled to Holland with it for performances.

Kevin graduated from McMaster University with a B.A. and from Windsor University with a master's in marketing. He had a propensity for marketing and worked in the marketing department of a number of companies.

In 1989, he married Vicki Fenn, who was also in marketing. Vicki was the perfect match for Kevin, as her personality and demeanour were quite opposite to his, with her calm, thoughtful approach to life. She has a very pleasant personality, with a lovely sense of humour, which came in handy at times, I'm sure, dealing with a more assertive and at times impulsive husband. From their marriage came forth two wonderful sons, Brook and Taylor.

## A TRIBUTE TO KEVIN'S WIFE AND SONS

It can be challenging for a widow to hold everything together when left with the full responsibility of caring for two adolescent sons, but no mother could have fulfilled that role better than Vicki did. She has made it all look so seamless, continuing to take an interest in every aspect of the boys' lives. And the boys in turn have responded beautifully to the loss of their dear dad, whom they loved and respected so deeply. The eldest, Brook, is now an honours graduate in business and has found excellent full-time employment. Taylor continues as a university student, also in the business course.

## COPING WITH A SON'S LOSS

I miss Kevin beyond words! He was cast in the same mould as his dad—creative, caring, generous, light-spirited, mischievous, gregarious, loquacious, athletic, joke-teller, punner, confident, organized, designer and builder, inquisitive, a little argumentative, a get-up-and-at-it guy—and, most of all, he loved life to the full. I miss his morning phone calls, always commencing with the same question:

"Well, Father, what do you have on your platter for today?" And then we would always get into a punning game. Kevin could lighten anyone's day, and all who knew him will attest to that. His life was the epitome of this Nully Nugget: "Life is too short to take it too seriously." And speaking of my Nully Nuggets—my sayings—Kevin often encouraged me to print them in a book. How amazing that his wish is now coming true in this book. He must be smiling.

How do parents comfort themselves when they lose a child—of any age—to death? How do you get over it? The simple answer is, *you never get over the trauma;* you can only *work through it* the best you can, through God's grace (2 Corinthians 12:9) and His strength (Philippians 4:13). Here are some other things I have found helpful:

1. I thank God for the wonderful memories.
2. I thank God that someday we will meet again in eternity.
3. I thank God that his life is being lived out through the lives of his wonderful sons he left behind!
4. I try to be a comfort to others who have lost a child, and that brings to mind another of my Nully Nuggets: "The best way to bear your own burdens is to help someone else bear theirs."

# CHAPTER 6

# "LOSS" OF MY BELOVED WIFE THROUGH ALZHEIMER'S

## A FAIRY-TALE ROMANCE

The story of how Carolyn and I came to be husband and wife and soulmates is indeed a fairy-tale story.

In June of 1976 I preached at the anniversary service at Stanley Avenue Baptist Church in Hamilton—where I had been the pastor for 10 years and where Carolyn's cousin Jan Spring was the organist. A certain schoolteacher at Forest Heights Collegiate Institute in Kitchener would ofttimes spend a weekend with her cousin Jan and her husband, Bill, and they would take her to church with them. In fact I remember the beautiful white coat she wore and her warm smile when I shook her hand on her way out of church. Who could ever forget Carolyn's beautiful smile?

I had been invited by my brother Howie and his wife, Ivy, to have lunch with them before returning to Barrie. After lunch, as I was putting my coat on, Ivy said to me, "Oh, Ern, Jan and I know the very person for you"—meaning of course the person who would become my wife.

Well, it was like an epiphany, and I replied, "Who would that be?"

She replied, "Carolyn Cameron." And then it registered: Yes, the lady with the white coat, the warm smile and the warm handshake.

On the drive back to Barrie that Sunday afternoon I could hardly contain my excitement, as I had the feeling that this was the person God was going to bring into my life as my wife and into the lives of my boys as their new mother. I had made the decision (as I was only 47 years old and in excellent health) to seek God's guidance in relation to dating again, hopefully leading to marriage to the person of God's choice.

As it had not been long since the boys had lost their dear mom (just three months), I planned on keeping them informed about any dates that I would be having. We had a very warm and caring relationship, always having each other's best interests at heart. How blessed I was that my sons looked at the future of my life in such positive terms! I knew that they were willing to go along with whatever would bring happiness into their dad's life again. Not every parent is blessed like that when their spouse passes on and they bring someone else into the relationship, more often than not having to do with financial matters and the will.

I have shared with people (ofttimes in my sermons) that I had set out seven criteria for the person coming into my life, number one being that she had be a dedicated follower of our Lord. I have revealed the other six criteria to only family members and close friends. What do you think some of them should have been? Discuss it with others and see what you come up with, just for fun.

## THE CAMERON FAMILY
The Cameron family owned and operated a huge farm on the northern outskirts of Barrie. They were not congregants of my parish but would often attend when we had outstanding musicians or preachers visit. Because of my photographic memory, I remembered well the young son who attended with them and in particular the little sweet and shy daughter with the warm smile and handshake. Who would ever have believed—at that point—that I was looking at and shaking hands with the very person who would one day become my beloved wife, the new mother to my boys, and the mother of our son Eric? Oh, the ironies of life! Amazing and awesome!

## PLANS LEADING TO A FIRST DATE
I now felt that Carolyn Cameron was God's choice to be my future wife, but with her living and teaching in Kitchener, how was I going to bring this feeling to fruition? There's an old saying that "Love finds a way," and it surely did!

## MAKING THE PHONE CALL
I was sitting in my office at the aluminum company in Barrie, where I was employed as the general manager. It was a lovely warm Wednesday in June (my favourite month) when I felt a strong urge to phone Carolyn's cousin Jan Spring and ask for her thoughts about me inviting Carolyn on a dinner date. Jan responded enthusiastically, "Yes, I think that's a great idea, because at a recent

ladies retreat that we attended together, Carolyn asked me, 'Have you heard from Ernie lately?'" That seemed to me like a confirmation that God was leading in that direction. Jan gave me Carolyn's phone number, I thanked her for her advice, and we said our goodbyes.

As soon as I got off the phone, my heart started to beat at a quickened pace. I felt really excited about the possibility of going on a date with Carolyn and what that might lead to.

So that evening (with the boys out and about) I picked up the phone and dialed Carolyn's number. The "Hello" came from one of the sweetest voices I have ever heard on the phone. I responded with "Carolyn, this is Ernie Nullmeyer." She immediately apologized for how long it had taken her to get to the phone as she had been in the shower, having just returned from her horseback riding lesson. I thought to myself, *Wow, anyone who is that thoughtful is the person for me.*

As an icebreaker, I said, "Carolyn, Jan mentioned that she had been on a retreat with you last weekend, and I understand that you both had a wonderful time."

"Yes," she said, "we sure did!"

I continued, "Carolyn, I am planning to get tickets to a musical that takes place at the Georgian Theatre in three weeks, and I was wondering if you would like to be my guest."

"Sure," she responded, "I would love to do that."

I thought to myself, *I love her spirit of enthusiasm; that's the kind of person I need and want in my life.*

Then she added, "I am planning on spending the next three weekends with Mom and Dad, so that will work out well." (I wonder if she was planting a seed.)

I said, "Wonderful. I'll call you again closer to the event, and we'll work out the details."

"That will be great," she replied, and we said our goodbyes.

As soon as I hung up, I thought, *If Carolyn is coming to Barrie this weekend, why don't I take her out on a date this coming Friday?* I phoned back (again hearing that sweet voice) and said, "Carolyn, as you're coming to Barrie this weekend, would you like to go out for dinner with me on Friday evening?"

"Sure," she responded enthusiastically, "I would love to do that."

"Great. I will pick you up at your parents' place." We said goodbye and hung up.

## TELLING MY SONS

I could hardly wait until the boys arrived home to tell them what I was up to on the phone that evening. They both smiled broadly, as they wanted their dad (who had been through a lot with the ill health and passing away of their mom) to be smiling and laughing again. They said, "That's great, Dad; go for it!" What wonderful understanding and caring sons!

Later in our courtship, Carolyn told me that when she went to school the day after my phone call, colleagues told her she was glowing. Yes, this beautiful person, Carolyn Cameron, was about to find the right man, for whom she had prayed for quite a few years and whom she had not yet found at 34 years of age. I have since thanked God for that.

## FEELINGS OF EXCITEMENT

The next two days, I couldn't get it off my mind that I would be going out on a date and with the person who would probably become my beloved wife and the stepmother of my beloved sons.

## FIRST DATE

On the Friday evening of our first date Carolyn was waiting out on the porch with her dear mom, who was almost as excited as her daughter, both having a hunch that this romance was going to lead to marriage—and I think they both hoped so, as I certainly did! We went to a restaurant in Alliston for dinner. As we look back, neither one of us remembers what (if anything) we ate, but we do remember looking into each other's eyes with feelings of excitement that this first date would not be the last, and it certainly wasn't.

We spent much of the following weekend together, including attending church on Sunday. The next Friday, which was originally going to be our first date, we went to the theatre, and we again spent much of the weekend together. If there is such a thing as falling in love, it was surely happening to us.

## SUMMER OF '76 AND COURTSHIP

During the summer of 1976, Carolyn lived with her parents, and we were involved in all kinds of fun activities, as well as talking seriously about our future relationship. Through much discussion and prayer we came to believe that God had brought us together and that it was His will that in due time we would be married. So we decided in August (six weeks after our first date) to get engaged. I met with her parents to inform them of our plans, and they said they were delighted that their beloved daughter Carolyn had finally found the right man to marry. I'll always remember her dad's few words: "Ernie, you are getting a very special lady." No truer words ever have or could have been spoken. No one who has known my beloved Carolyn has ever heard a negative word spoken about her. She and her beloved mom—Jean Lois Cameron—are two of the most beautiful ladies the world has ever known.

## SONS' AND SIBLINGS' REACTIONS

Someone might wonder what my sons thought about all this going on in their dad's life and at such a quick pace. I had decided—because of the close relationship I had always had with them—to keep them informed about what was going on, and they accepted it all with great grace. They knew what I had experienced with the long-term illness and passing of their mom, and they just wanted what was best for me. How blessed can a dad get?

And what about the reactions of my eight sisters and brother? One evening I sat down at my typewriter (remember those?) and typed each one a personal letter to let them know about my plans.

A couple of my sisters thought it was all happening too soon, but eventually they came to realize, along with my other siblings, what a wise decision I had made and what a beautiful person I was marrying. Can you imagine the scene when Carolyn met all of my nine siblings and their spouses at a bridal shower sponsored by my sisters? She handled it all in her usual graceful manner.

## ENGAGEMENT

On a very warm day in August of 1976, we went to a jewellery store in downtown Barrie and together picked out a lovely (but not over-the-top-expensive) ring, and that evening I had the joy of placing it on her lovely finger as we looked lovingly into each other's eyes and knew beyond a shadow of a doubt that this would be a dream marriage. As the song says, "Your eyes met mine, and we were falling in love." We had already fallen in love, and deeply!

## THE INTERVAL

Carolyn returned to Kitchener for the September through December semester to complete her twelve-year teaching career at Forest Heights Collegiate. She returned to Barrie then to live with her parents on the farm and to continue our courtship. This was another opportunity for us to get to know each other at a deeper level and to make our wedding plans.

## THE WEDDING

After much discussion and prayer we decided that our wedding would be held on January 29, 1977, in Yorkminster Baptist Church in Toronto. Well, the last weekend of January often brings on the worst storm of the year. It surely did that year. (I've often said to people that we were married in the midst of a storm but had smooth sailing during the years of our marriage.)

We were supposed to travel to Toronto on the Friday and have the rehearsal that evening. However, that was not to be, as a winter storm began blowing in about noon on Friday and was not to abate until early the next morning. All roads to Toronto were shut down. It was a very emotionally disturbing experience for Carolyn, but I kept assuring her on the phone that everything would work out fine and we would travel to Toronto on Saturday morning. She was also worried—and naturally so—that the guests wouldn't be able to make it. Again I assured her that those who were supposed to would. (In fact it turned out that only two guests were not able to get there.)

## A MOST UNUSUAL WEDDING REHEARSAL

On Saturday morning, when we were getting ready for the rehearsal at the church, the secretary told us that Dr. Gladstone would not be able to make it in time for the rehearsal. He was the guest preacher at a men's retreat in Aurora, and traffic was slow. So what would we do about the rehearsal? Well, it so happened that the groom had performed numerous rehearsals as part of the hundreds of weddings he had conducted. So the groom—Rev. Ernest Nullmeyer—performed what was perhaps the oddest wedding rehearsal ever.

It turned out to be a lot of fun, as the groom/minister went back and forth from the wedding line to the front of the wedding party. Sometimes as we look back in life, we see that situations that looked like they were going to be a disaster turned out just fine and are a cause for laughter.

## A CLOSE CALL

About 30 minutes before the wedding was to commence, Dr. Gladstone—to the relief of all (and especially the bride)—turned up. He then performed a beautiful ceremony. The bride's attendants were her sisters Mary and Nancy, a long-time friend, and—who else but Jan Spring, her cousin and our bridge-builder.

My groomsmen were my brother Howard and a long-time Christian friend.

The ushers were none other than my very own wonderful sons, who did an amazing job!

## RECEPTION

The reception was held in a nearby hotel and went off without a hitch. We included in the program a number of Christian songs sung by a former elder at Stanley Avenue Baptist, "Love Divine, All Loves Excelling" and "Channels Only." The guests all said at the end what a joy it was for them to have participated in such a beautiful and Christ-exalting wedding and reception.

## AMAZING GOOD NEWS!

Carolyn and I were not sure whether or not we should even think about having a child. We prayed about it, and we agreed that even though I was approaching 50 years of age and she was in her mid-thirties, it would be wonderful for her to bear and bring forth a child. I knew that I would be excited beyond words to become a parent again.

## BIRTH OF OUR BELOVED SON

However, Carolyn had a medical condition that made it doubtful that she could bear a child. So it was all in God's hands (well, mostly!), and on May 25, 1979, in the Royal Victoria Hospital in Barrie, Carolyn brought forth her firstborn (and lastborn), a beautiful baby boy whom we named Eric Cameron. What wonderful years we have enjoyed with Eric! He has brought innumerable joys into our lives, including his lovely wife, Leanne, and their adorable twin daughters. Who would ever have believed when I was going through the painful and stressful years of Marion's illness and demise that in due time I would experience such indescribable joy?

## STORM CLOUDS FORMING

Here's another Nully Nugget: "Life is not simple, smooth or stationary." The truth of that maxim was to become a huge reality in the life of our family.

How often when we are enjoying a picnic on a glorious summer afternoon do we suddenly notice storm clouds in the distance and have to bring the fun to an unexpected end? That is somewhat a metaphor for what was about to happen in Carolyn and Eric's life and mine, and eventually in the lives of all of our family. I was the only one to notice those early storm clouds, and it was very painful to see it happening and to keep it to myself until sometime in the future when other family members would become aware of what was occurring in Carolyn's life and brain.

## EARLY SIGNS OF ALZHEIMER'S

It was a lovely snowy day in Barrie with the maple trees in the woods behind our beautiful country home decked in their winter finest. Having eaten supper, Carolyn and I were washing the dishes together. We did have a dishwasher, but we seldom used it as Carolyn didn't like the noise it made or the water it wasted. Being brought up on the farm as she was—in fact on the very farm surrounding our home—she believed that water was never to be wasted. As we carried on our domestic task, Carolyn turned to me and asked me a question. I replied, "My darling, I just answered that question for you." I shall never forget the painful look in her eyes and on her face. She again turned to me, and she said, "Please don't say that to me again." I will never know exactly what that statement meant. But for me, having had as a pastor considerable exposure to those who were experiencing the heart-wrenching skill- and dignity-robbing disease of Alzheimer's, the dreaded thought went through my mind: *Could this be happening to my beloved Carolyn?* My silent prayer was "Dear God, don't let it be; anything but Alzheimer's!" The desperate words of this prayer were a result of seeing many parishioners and several sisters with this devastating, usually long-term, disease and my conclusion that it was among the worst—if not the worst—of any disease. Now, after all the times I have visited Carolyn in the long-term-care facility and witnessed the sounds and sights of patients with Alzheimer's, I am more convinced of this than ever. (See my personal thoughts on Alzheimer's at the end of this chapter.)

I decided that I would not share my suspicion with anyone, hoping that I was wrong. However, as I continued to monitor her behaviour, my suspicion was more and more validated. She was having difficulty comprehending and retaining what she was reading and would read the same page over repeatedly. She got frustrated trying to operate the TV remote control, not remembering how to do it from one time to the next. Financial matters were becoming more and more difficult for her to comprehend and remember, and she expressed over and over her (unnecessary) fear of not having enough money if she had to go into a nursing home. (Was that fear part of what was happening to her mentally?) I noticed that her computer skills were declining, and she was becoming more and more frustrated trying to deal with it. She was spending more and more time in bed during the day, perhaps as an escape from not feeling able to deal with what was happening to her. I will never know how aware Carolyn was at that time that something life-changing was happening in her brain. It really wouldn't have made any difference one way or the other, as we just carried on our lives as normally as possible and having a litany of good times, together and with family and friends. At that stage, we were enjoying our walks along the bay, having coffee at our favourite spot with friends, attending church and taking in concerts. However, I noticed that no matter what activity we were enjoying together, her attention span was continually decreasing. When I asked her to have friends in for dinner or even tea, she would say "No, I don't feel up to that." That was not "normal" for Carolyn, as she had always been such a gregarious person in whatever social situation she found herself in.

## A BIG MOVE

About this time I was beginning to feel that taking care of a large house plus the surrounding acreage was too much for me, having turned 80 and still wanting to have the energy to golf and downhill ski. So we decided to move into a condo. It was a beautiful condo overlooking Lake Simcoe. While preparing for the move I became aware of Carolyn's limitations in concentrating on making decisions about the necessary downsizing. Of course that is always a formidable task for anyone, but there was more to it than that. Only with the help of her sister were we able to get the task completed, and we made our move to the condo.

It was here that I noticed with greater clarity that something drastic was happening to Carolyn's health in general and memory in particular. She would sleep in every morning and then not feel capable of preparing meals, so either we ate out or I did the meal preparation.

After two years in the condo I decided that we needed to be living closer to one of our sons, so we began to prepare for a move to Waterloo Region, where we would be close to our son Eric and the twin girls who were on the way. We moved to a lovely seniors' community in St. Jacobs and enjoyed it there for three years. However, during this time I became aware of even more drastic changes in Carolyn's behaviour.

## MORE SIGNS

When Carolyn was driving, more often than not she would be hesitant about which way to turn. She was always a very capable driver and comprehended directions very well, so once again my suspicions were authenticated. As I continued to monitor her cognitive ability, I noticed that she was not able to operate the TV remote, and when we were playing Scrabble (which we had played nightly for years) partway through she would put her tiles back in the box and say "I'm not up to that anymore."

One day when she seemed to be spending a lot of time in the kitchen just to get tea for us, I slipped in to see what the delay was, and she literally fell into my arms and started to weep.

When I asked her what was wrong, she said (and I have this verbatim in my journal), "Darling, I've reached an impasse in my life; I don't even know how to get tea anymore." I took her in my arms, and we had a good weep together, the first of innumerable times when we would repeat that scenario.

One Saturday evening Eric and Leanne and the twins brought in a meal to have supper with us. As we were setting the table, Eric drew me aside and said, "Dad, do you think Mom could be in the early stages of Alzheimer's?"

I asked why he was asking that. His response was "When I asked her to place the drinking glasses on the table, she was confused as to what to do with them."

I then looked him in the eye and replied, "Eric, I have been suspicious of Mom being in the early stages of Alzheimer's for almost five years."

## TIME FOR A DOCTOR'S APPOINTMENT

It was time, obviously, to make an appointment with our family physician and relate what had been happening in Carolyn's life. Our doctor decided that Carolyn should take a memory test, which involved simply memorizing a number of objects on a tray and then relating that information back to the nurse. We returned the next week for the report, and that was when our doctor looked into her eyes (with a look of sadness) and said, "Carolyn, I am sorry to say that you failed the memory test, and I am going to have to ask the Ministry of Transportation to revoke your driver's licence." What a bombshell! And of course it caused Carolyn to break down. She had been driving since the age of 16 and had never been involved in an accident of her doing. Our doctor (such a caring person) wheeled her chair over to Carolyn, placed her hands on Carolyn's legs and said, "Some things in life we just don't have any control over." Truer words could not have been spoken, and those words express my theological understanding as to why bad things happen to good people (even people as good and beautiful as my beloved Carolyn). I elucidate on that subject in appendix 1.

## TESTS AND CONFIRMATION

The doctor then advised us that Carolyn should go to the memory clinic at Freeport Medical Centre in Kitchener for a more in-depth assessment. On April 26, 2013, Eric and I took his mom to the clinic. Following a number of assessments, the physician in charge said that Carolyn needed to be admitted to the clinic for further assessments. It was a very scary time for Carolyn, as she didn't know what exactly would be involved. Thank God we were able to afford a private room, as the behaviour of many of the patients was close to intolerable. It turned out that this exposure would somewhat prepare her for what would eventually come in long-term care.

She went through a myriad of tests, including many at the Grand River imaging clinic, and after seven weeks she was diagnosed by a geriatric research scientist as having Lewy body dementia (a combination of Alzheimer's and Parkinson's).

Following Carolyn's discharge we continued to live in St. Jacobs until I could no longer cope with all that was now involved in caring for her along with all the domestic responsibilities, so we moved into a retirement residence. That eased the domestic burden for me but not the caring burden, as I had to do an increasing number of tasks for her, including bathing her. She didn't want to eat in the dining room, feeling embarrassed about her memory problem, so I had to bring all the meals to our apartment.

## LONG-TERM CARE

I felt it was time to think about moving Carolyn into long-term care (LTC). She was assessed by the Community Care access representative, and the decision was that we would get Carolyn into LTC as soon as possible. So in April of 2014, she was admitted to LTC, where at the time of writing this she continues to decline and at a more rapid pace.

Every morning as I rise for the day's activities I thank God that I have the physical health and energy as well as the mental acumen to visit Carolyn every day to help her with eating, push her around the facility in her wheelchair and prepare her for bed. At every visit she apologizes to me for "causing all this trouble" (which of course is not how I feel), tells me repeatedly how much she loves me and then asks me to just hold her. I count it a privilege to be able to give such TLC to such a beautiful person, who still shows forth every day her sweet smile and sweet spirit. When Carolyn's earthly journey will end, and how much psychological pain we will have to suffer in the meantime, only God knows. However, we do know that when that happens, she will commence her eternal journey and be in the presence of her Lord and Saviour, whom she has loved and served with passion. Until her earthly departure, I will be there for her, always ready and willing to hug her and hold her.

## GOD'S PROVISION OF A SPECIAL CAREGIVER-COMPANION

The Psalmist declared that the Lord—who is our Shepherd—will provide everything for us that we need (Psalm 23:1). We certainly witnessed that promise come to fruition in the person who would eventually become a support and companion for Carolyn. Our son Eric decided that it would be a good idea for us to hire a cleaning lady, as Carolyn was no longer up that task and I had my hands full (in fact overloaded) with caring for Carolyn and trying to have some life of my own. It was not safe at this stage of her illness to leave her alone. Eric noticed a little tiny ad in a coffee shop paper, contacted the lady, and brought her to our home. We hired her as our cleaning lady, but little did we know at the time that she would become the very best caregiver and companion for Carolyn that we could have imagined. God does exciting things for us in our lives if our spiritual eyes are open to see them.

I had hired a number of personal support workers (PSWs) from a couple of companies. They were lovely ladies and always did their best, but the plan didn't work out for Carolyn for two reasons:

1. A different one could turn up every day, and that was terribly confusing for Carolyn.
2. They tried too hard to stimulate her in many different ways, as they are trained to do, and that became very frustrating for Carolyn.

So, what to do? I asked our cleaning lady, Anne Smithers, if she would be interested in becoming Carolyn's caregiver-companion. She had already thought about the idea and bought into it immediately. We hired her at first for just the times when I had to go out or was involved in an activity at the retirement residence where we were living at the time. When Carolyn was admitted to the long-term care facility, I was spending many hours with her every day of the week. Eventually I realized that I couldn't keep that up and have any time for myself, so I hired Anne for a certain number of hours every day. It has worked out beautifully for her, for Carolyn and for me. Anne is a very gentle, warm, wise and caring person and was indeed, I believe, sent to us from God to eventually become not just a caregiver-companion for Carolyn but also a personal friend.

Our Good Shepherd knows how to provide for us, and He certainly has in the person of Anne Smithers.

## CAROLYN'S AUTOBIOGRAPHY

In preparation for giving her speech at her 70th birthday celebration, planned by Eric and Leanne and held at a golf club in Milton, Carolyn asked me to write her thoughts down and then print them for her. The following was what I wrote down and printed with her approval.

### Three Score Years and Ten
It's hard to believe that I have arrived at that biblical age—seven decades of God's blessings upon my life.

#### THE FIRST DECADE
The joy of being a student in a one-room schoolhouse, just up the concession from our farm home outside of Barrie, and having excellent, caring teachers.

#### THE SECOND DECADE
Having a handsome 18-year-old Mennonite teacher for grade 8, then on to high school, enjoying every subject and having the privilege of playing the saxophone in an award-winning band, and even travelling to Holland by ship and flying home for my first time in an airplane.

I also had the pleasure and honour of performing with the band before the queen at Gravenhurst. As I look back at those teen years, I realize how blessed I was to have two loving, caring and very wise parents who helped make my adolescent years go smoothly.

#### THE THIRD DECADE
Studying French and Latin at the University of Toronto preparing for my career as a language teacher and then having the privilege and pleasure of teaching those subjects to my high school students for 12 years at Forest Heights Collegiate, Kitchener.

#### THE FOURTH DECADE
Four exciting highlights:

1. A handsome, God-fearing, fun-loving gentleman by the name of Ernest came into my life. I can remember driving to school the Monday following our first date in Alliston and realizing that I was just beaming and smiling from ear to ear. The first colleague I ran into said, "Carolyn, you are glowing; it must have been a wonderful date." I replied, "It sure was!"
2. Becoming engaged to the man of my dreams, planning our wedding together, and having such a beautiful wedding.
3. Building our new home in the country, on property given to us by my generous parents, and having the joy of living just around the corner from Mom and Dad.
4. Welcoming into our lives God's amazing gift of a beautiful baby boy, whom we named Eric Cameron.

#### THE FIFTH DECADE
Having the joy of being a stay-at-home mom and caring for our beloved son Eric until his entrance into kindergarten and then retraining to teach French at the elementary level in Elmvale.

#### THE SIXTH DECADE
Many wonderful trips together. For years I made them on my own, but now I had my very own travelling companion, and...a man to carry my bags. (Ha! Ha!) How wonderful! And then two big moves: first from our beautiful home in the country into

the city of Barrie and to a lovely condo overlooking scenic Kempenfelt Bay, then to a lovely bungalow in the beautiful tourist town of St. Jacobs. How blessed we are to live so close to our son Eric and his wife, Leanne, and our newest grandchildren, twins Kyla and Lily. How blessed I am to be called "Grandma" by ten of the most wonderful grandchildren one could ever ask for.

### THE SEVENTH DECADE?

Only our Heavenly Father knows what is ahead! As the Psalmist wrote, our times are in God's hands (Psalm 31:15) and *"Our days may come to seventy years, or eighty, if our strength endures"* (Psalm 90:10). Isn't it wonderful that a light shines upon our lives—no matter how dark they may become at times—when we read the following Psalm:

*Whoever dwells in the shelter of the Most High will rest in the shadow of the Almighty. I will say of the LORD, "He is my refuge and my fortress, my God, in whom I trust."…He will cover you with his feathers, and under his wings you will find refuge; his faithfulness will be your shield and rampart.* (Psalm 91:1–4)

Along with those strengthening thoughts, I thank God that it is also strengthening to be surrounded by and supported by so many who are there to be my support: my beloved husband; my loving, caring sons and their wives; my precious grandchildren; my sisters and brother and their spouses; my close friends and my Great Shepherd.

Author's note: Although I was aware at this time that my beloved soulmate Carolyn was in the early stages of Alzheimer's, I do not know how aware she was of that. One would almost conclude that she must have had an inkling or even premonition of that when she wrote, "Only our Heavenly Father knows what is ahead!" Praise God, He does, and we know with assurance that He will always be there for us, His children. Isaiah the Prophet wrote, *"I, the LORD, have called you in righteousness; I will take hold of your hand"* (Isaiah 42:6) and *"Do not be afraid, for I am with you"* (Isaiah 43:5).

One of Carolyn's favourite choruses when she was growing up and throughout her life was "Safe Am I in the Hollow of God's Hands" by Mildred Leightner Dillon. This song reminded Carolyn of the sense of security we have when we commit every aspect of our lives into the hands of our Heavenly Father. How often we hear someone say "I know it's in good hands." That expresses perfectly how we can feel as God's children.

## PERSONAL THOUGHTS ON ALZHEIMER'S

All who have played a primary role in the care of a person (especially a close loved one who has an irremediable disease) will know something of the psychological pain experienced by both patient and caregiver. This is particularly true in the case of a patient with Alzheimer's, as I have experienced in caring for my beloved wife Carolyn during the past many years of her declining health. I have also been exposed to it often as the brother of three sisters with the disease and as a pastor tending to the spiritual needs of many congregants.

Alzheimer's is a memory-robbing, skill-robbing, dignity-robbing disease and culminates in the patients becoming as dependent as they were in their infancy. I am witnessing that now with Carolyn, and it is a heartbreaking, heart-wrenching sight to have to behold! Unlike with many types of cancer, there is no medication or surgery for it, it never goes into remission and it is (depending on the general health of the patient) very long-term and painfully dragged out.

If there is one disease for which a patient should be able to declare advance consent for assisted dying, it is Alzheimer's! I am 100 percent in favour of that becoming legislation in our country, and the sooner the better, especially if I become a victim of Alzheimer's. How often my beloved soulmate Carolyn and I have wept together (until there were no more tears to flow) because of the intensely deep psychological pain she was going through, and actually we are *both* going through. She would share with me her feelings in statements like "Just dig a hole and bury me"; "I just want to die"; "Isn't there something the doctors can do for me?"; "I've had enough" and "Pray that God will end this soon."

I am not a neuroscientist, but since Carolyn became afflicted with Alzheimer's I have spent a lot of time and energy researching the subject. In an article about University of Toronto neuroscientist Graham Collingridge, reporter Joseph Hall writes, "Memory is the indispensable human faculty."[1] One of the best books I have read on the subject of Alzheimer's is *The Memory Clinic: Stories of Hope and Healing for Alzheimer's Patients and Their Families,* by Tiffany Chow, a behavioural neurologist and senior scientist at Baycrest Health Centre in Toronto.[2] Dr. Chow includes a chapter on caregivers that I am sure everyone caring for a patient with the disease will find very helpful. I read the chapter every so often to make sure I am staying on track as Carolyn's primary caregiver.

## TIPS FOR VISITING PATIENTS WITH ALZHEIMERS

I have made close to 1,000 visits to spend time with my beloved Carolyn in a long-term-care facility, visited many times with several of my sisters when they were in LTC with Alzheimer's and visited parishioners with chronic illnesses on numerous occasions during my pastoral ministry. These experiences have given

---

[1] Joseph Hall, "Inspiration and luck drove Graham Collingridge, winner of Brain Prize," *Toronto Star,* March 14, 2016, https://www.thestar.com/news/insight/2016/03/14/inspiration-and-luck-drove-graham-collingridge-winner-of-brain-prize.html.

[2] Tiffany Chow, *The Memory Clinic: Stories of Hope and Healing for Alzheimer's Patients and Their Families* (Toronto: Viking, 2013).

me the opportunity to make many observations about life in a LTC facility. Many of these observations are not pleasant ones, but the one I want to emphasize here is how many patients rarely receive a visit from a family member or friend. I do not of course know all the reasons why that is so, but I am going to speculate as to why it may be:

1. Seeing one's loved one or close friend in such a state is too great an emotional pain to bear.
2. The patient will not remember the visit even moments after.
3. It's awkward and painful to know how to carry on a conversation.

These all seem like valid and justifiable reasons, but perhaps if the loved ones and friends of the patient were more informed as to how to deal with the situation, it might make a difference.

Here are my thoughts about overcoming the reluctance to visit with a loved one or friend in a long-term-care facility:

1. Remember that an Alzheimer's patient lives *only* in the *now*. Do not expect him or her to recall anything from the past or to be able to think about the future.
2. Remember that—whatever the cognizant state of the patient may be—there is still a soul, a spirit, inside that body that can be ministered to.
3. Remember that the patient will usually respond to a loving touch or, better still, a hug and a hold.
4. Assisting the patient at mealtime is a great way to get him or her to respond to you. It is very possible that such an engagement will trigger the times when you had coffee, tea or a meal together.
5. Remember the Golden Rule and apply it to a possible someday when you may be in that situation, and then ask yourself if you would want to be abandoned by loved ones or friends at such a time. Even though each and every visit with my beloved soulmate Carolyn gets more emotionally painful, I remind myself that if our situations were reversed, Carolyn would be there for me every day as I am for her.
6. Remember that this should not be about you, your feelings or your discomfort; it should be about meeting the needs of the patient. It is what is known as ministry or giving of ourselves to reach out and meet the needs of those less fortunate than we are.
7. Remember, as my Nully Nugget states it, "The purpose of life is to be a blessing to others; that will bring happiness to us and to others."

May the God of all grace give *us* the grace to be there for those who need us, and may we be able to say with the prophet Habakkuk,

*Though the fig tree does not bud and there are no grapes on the vines, though the olive crop fails and the fields produce no food, though there are no sheep in the pen and no cattle in the stalls, yet will I be joyful in the LORD, I will be joyful in God my Savior. The sovereign LORD is my strength; he makes my feet like the feet of a deer, he enables me to tread on the heights.* (Habakkuk 3:17–19)

## IN GOD'S STRONG HANDS

When Carolyn and I visited the obstetrics ward to lay eyes on, for the very first time, our recently born twin granddaughters, it was hard to believe how tiny they were—just around three pounds each. Our son Eric lovingly and gently picked up one of them and held her in the palm of his strong and mighty hand. What safety! What security! And that is a picture of us—as God's weak and dependent children—experiencing safety and security in the strong and mighty hand of our loving Heavenly Father. Jesus put it this way:

> *"My sheep listen to my voice; I know them, and they follow me. I give them eternal life, and they shall never perish; no one will snatch them out of my hand. My Father, who has given them to me, is greater than all; no one can snatch them out of my Father's hand."* (John 10:27–29)

That's safety! That's security!

And that's the glorious and comforting assurance for me as Carolyn's soulmate and for our family as we watch helplessly the devastating effects that Alzheimer's is having on the personality and behaviour of even one so gentle, so gracious, as our beloved Carolyn. Praise God, she is in God's hands!

The North Toronto house I was born in on September 11, 1928. My parents had to sell the house at a huge loss in 1929 when the Great Depression started. We lived in old rented houses after that.

Keelesdale Baptist Church, where I spent much of my childhood and adolescence

This is the grocery store where I worked Friday evenings until 11:00 p.m. and Saturdays while I was in high school. I stocked shelves, filled phone orders and delivered them to customers' homes.

Dressed in my new suit bought for my 18th birthday by my sister Marjorie, 1946

The new building dedication at Emmanuel Baptist, June 16, 1957, was a family affair with my mom and Marion (front row), my brother and eight sisters (back row). Left to right: Marjorie, Joan, Rose, Irene, Howard, Ellen (eldest), Hilma, Gladys and Mary

Stanley Avenue Baptist, Hamilton, Ontario, 1970

"Boom-Boom" Nullmeyer (far right) with Revs. Al Smith and Cecil Brenn ready to take on the Barrie City Council in 1958; proceeds of the event went to Barrie and District Christmas Cheer

In Norway, homeplace of my dad, 1987

A quiet evening at home in Barrie, 1992

The "Big Day" for Carolyn and me, January 29, 1977, Toronto, Ontario

Dunn's River, Jamaica, 2000

Volunteer work in Barrie with a mere handful of the thousands of toys donated each year for the less fortunate children of Barrie and District, 2001

Citizen of the Year award, Barrie, Ontario, 1995

Skiing in Sunshine, Banff, 1986

No "Hole-in-One" yet!

Four "fun-loving" sons and their "fun-loving" dad; Father's Day, June 16, 2005

Barry and Cindy's wedding, October 22, 1983,
in Stony Plain, Alberta

Barry and Cindy's daughters,
Savannah and Caite

Brad and Cathy's wedding, October 8, 1983, in Barrie, Ontario

Brad and Cathy's children, Ashley, Andrew, Jocelyn and Ali

Kevin and Vicki's wedding, June 10, 1989, in Oakville, Ontario

Kevin and Vicki's sons, Taylor and Brook

Eric and Leanne's wedding, August 29, 2003

Eric and Leanne's daughters,
Kyla and Lily

We are one big, happy family, August 3, 2008. Left to right: Jocelyn, Savannah, Barry, Caite, Bradley, Ernie, Eric, Kevin, and Brook (back row); Andrew, Cindy, Cathy, Carolyn, Leanne, Vicki, and Ashley (middle row); Ali, and Taylor (front row).

Preaching at Bethel Community Church, Barrie, Ontario in 2006 at 78 years of age; 60 years after my first sermon at age eighteen

# PART TWO

## TRAUMAS RELIEVED

*In all these things we are more than conquerors through Him who loved us.*
(Romans 8:37, NKJV)

*I can do all things through Christ who strengthens me.*
(Philippians 4:13, NKJV)

# Introduction

Now that I have articulated some of the most painful traumas of my life, under the title "Traumas Revealed," I move on to "Traumas Relieved." I want to share with you how I triumphed over the traumas of my life—with a clearer understanding of what the apostle Paul meant when he wrote, "*I can do all things through Christ who strengthens me*" (Philippians 4:13, NKJV)—and also how I have been enabled to deal with these traumas with a smile on my face, a sparkle in my eyes, a spring in my step, and, best of all, a song (or whistle) on my lips. Hopefully it will be a blessing in some little way to you as you deal with the painful vicissitudes of your life—past, present and future.

We have all faced circumstances that we *wished* we could have avoided. We may have even been envious of others who have not had to experience the kind of traumas we have had to endure. But "Life is not simple, smooth or stationary," as one of my Nully Nuggets puts it. Therefore, when those difficult, mean vicissitudes of life raise their ugly heads, we have a choice! We can either *react* negatively to them or *respond* positively! Life is full of choices, and when we make the *right* choices we will be enabled to live a life filled with joy and hope. That kind of life is about getting back up when we have fallen down. Ernest Hemingway wrote, "The world breaks everyone and afterward some are strong at the broken places."[3]

## FALLING DOWN AND GETTING BACK UP

When as a boy I was learning to skate, I kept falling. But I didn't *stay down*; I *got back up* and went at it again. Eventually I learned to be a very competent skater and a not-too-bad hockey player. At the age of 54, never having put skis on before, I took skiing lessons, along with my four-year-old son Eric. The first

---

[3] Ernest Hemingway, Brainy Quote, https://www.brainyquote.com/quotes/quotes/e/ernesthemi152913.html.

time down the hill—and countless times thereafter—I fell down. But I did not stay down; I got back up, which was no simple task, considering the length of the skis back in those days. In fact at first I was grateful to those competent skiers who would stop on the hill to give me a lift up to my feet. Eventually I became a competent skier, even skiing the Rockies only two years after I had first put skis on. I loved the feel of the warm sun and cold air on my cheeks while I sped down the mountain. But there were times when I was going too fast for my level of skill. That's how I broke my nose and almost fractured my hip, but that didn't stop me from continuing to ski; nor did it impede my speed. When I felt I was going down too fast, I would sing one of my mom's favourite hymn, "Nearer My God to Thee." Probably at times I wasn't far away from meeting Him face to face.

As children of God, it is not the desire of our loving Heavenly Father that the tough times of life should keep us down. He desires that by His grace and strength we will just keep getting back up and living our life to the full. That's what being triumphant means. May it always be your experience, and mine!

# CHAPTER 1

# TRAUMAS RELIEVED THROUGH THREE PRINCIPLES

## PRINCIPLE 1: ACCEPT THE CIRCUMSTANCES

All of us have had bad things happen in our lives, and more bad things will happen. It reminds me of the story of the man walking through the fairgrounds when he hears a vendor shouting, "Apples, the most delicious apples you've ever tasted!" The man goes up to the booth, hands his quarter to the vendor, and walks away, taking a bite of the apple. As he bites into it he discovers that the apple is rotten to the core. So with a mouth full of rotten apple he returns to the vendor and says, "Hey, Mac, that apple you sold me is rotten to the core." Replies the vendor, "Listen, buddy, you think you've got problems...I've got a whole bushel of 'em here."

Yes, we all have problems! I'm reminded of the lady who was walking to church on Easter Sunday, and the wind was blowing so hard that it was going to blow her lovely new Easter bonnet off. She prayed, "Lord, please change the wind around so my hat won't blow off." So God did. When walking home from church she was now facing the wind (that God had turned around), and she prayed, "Lord, just once more please turn the wind around." And God said, "My child, you have to learn to face the wind one way or the other."

## Bad Things Will Happen

It does seem that some people have more bad things happen in their lives than others. While some might describe their life as a bowl of cherries, others would describe theirs as "just the pits." Those in the latter group feel inclined to ask that question we began asking early in life: "Why?" Why did I have to lose a beloved son (through no fault of his own) and why did a friend have to lose four of her six children (all under different circumstances and through no fault of their own) when so many people I know have not had to go through the heartbreaking, heart-wrenching experience of being predeceased by a child? The simple answer is "I do not know," but the more profound answer is that they are just bad random acts of nature. If these (and others, like my first wife's seventeen-year battle with lupus and death at age 47 and my wife Carolyn's battle with Alzheimer's) were acts of God (as some Christians believe), that would make God a very unfair and unjust Heavenly Father, which I believe He is not. The Psalmist says, *"As a father has compassion on his children, so the LORD has compassion on those who fear him"* (Psalm 103:13). (For a more complete treatment of this subject, refer to appendix 1.)

### The Past Cannot Be Changed

If there is anything certain about life, it is that we cannot change the past. Too many people live as if they believe they can. There's an old Arab proverb that states, "You should write bad things that happen to you in the sand, so that the pain caused by them will be washed away with the flow of time." I would put it this way from my experience: The memory of the experience will not be washed away, but the pain of it will be mitigated by the good things that happen in your life. The apostle Paul put it this way: *"Whatever is true, whatever is noble, whatever is right, whatever is pure, whatever is lovely, whatever is admirable—if anything is excellent or praiseworthy—think about such things"* (Philippians 4:8). It is so easy to concentrate our thinking on the bad things that have happened to us. Allow me to encourage you to put the emphasis on the good things that have happened, are happening, and will happen in your life.

### We Have a Choice!

When bad things happen in our lives (and they will!) we have one of two choices: We can either react in a negative manner or respond in a positive manner. I have chosen the latter, as I realize I can either spend the rest of my life in the sinking sands of bitterness or get on with my life by moving on to practising the second principle. However, we cannot move on to the second principle until we have dealt with this first one, as there are *stepping* stones in the procedure, but no *skipping* stones. Yes, the old cliché has it right: "One step at a time."

It has been said that "Fretting about the past is like rocking on a rocking chair; it gives you something to do, but it doesn't get you anywhere." Each of us has to decide if we are going to accept the circumstances for what they are and then make a decision to move on to the next step. I hope you are ready for that. So let's move on together and believe that "Storms make oaks make deeper roots."

## PRINCIPLE 2: ADAPT TO THE CIRCUMSTANCES

Having made the decision to not get bogged down by what has happened in the past, we are ready for the next step. It is a big one, but not an impossible one. God has gifted each of us with an imaginative and creative spirit, and this is the time to put both of those attributes into action. We need to think creatively about what the possibilities are to get us through the painful experience. We also need to remember the promises of God's Word: "*In all your ways acknowledge Him, And He shall direct your paths*" (Proverbs 3:5–6, NKJV) and "*If any of you lacks wisdom, you should ask God, who gives generously to all without finding fault, and it will be given to you*" (James 1:5). I have put these two promises into action all of my life and can testify that they do work!

The choices we face are not always going to be to our complete liking, but that's just how life works. In my decorating business, when some staff members got all uptight about an onerous job we were tackling, I would say to them, "That's life in the trenches." I'm sure my dad and all the soldiers who fought in the world wars had to learn that. They did what they had to do, or, as I would put it, they adapted to the circumstances! I often think of the demanding situations surgeons must face on a day-to-day basis that they have no choice but to accept and adapt to, simply doing what has to be done for the good of the patient.

Is the process of adaptation easy or simple? It certainly hasn't been in my life, and it will not be in yours. Change is never easy, but when we face it head on realistically and prayerfully we will get through it and be better for it. That's been my experience, which is what part 2 of this book is all about!

### An Unusual Adaptation to Circumstances

I'm reminded of the man who—with great anticipation—went to a roast beef banquet. As he picked up his fork, he moaned, "Oh no." The man beside him asked what the problem was. He responded, "I left my dentures at home." "Oh," said the second man, "that's no problem." He pulled out a pair of dentures from his pocket and said, "Here, try these." So he did. "Oh my goodness," he said, "they are far too tight. I could never eat with them. But thanks anyway." "Oh, hang on," said the second man as he pulled out a set from another pocket, "try these." "Too loose," said the recipient, "but thanks anyway." "Well," said the other, "don't panic; I have one more pair for you to try." The man inserted them and said, "Perfect fit. Thank you so much, and where do you practice dentistry?" "Oh," said the denture-laden man, "I'm not a dentist. I'm a…funeral director." Yes, so often the solution to our problem is not one we would necessarily choose, but sometimes we just have to go with the flow, especially if we leave our dentures at home and have to adapt to the only solution available. The dear forgetful man ended up enjoying the roast beef dinner.

## PRINCIPLE 3: ADVANCE IN SPITE OF THE CIRCUMSTANCES

C. S. Lewis wrote, "Getting over a painful experience is like crossing monkey bars; you have to let go at some point to move forward."[4]

Like the former two principles, this one is also easier said than done. But that reaction can often just be a cop-out for not coming to grips with what action has to be taken in order to move on in life. Many people believe that everything will just work itself out without any effort on their part. It is true that there are some things we cannot do anything about (which is what principle 1 is about), and it would be nice if life were that simple, but it is not. This Nully Nugget is again appropriate here: "Life is not simple, smooth or stationary."

### Moving On!

In my pastoral ministry I have known many who have chosen to continue to live in the pit of self-pity and thus forgo many pleasures in life that could be theirs. I chose in every traumatic situation in my life not to go that route but rather to consider ways and means that I could move on and continue to live a life of joy and then, through my experience, bring inspiration and hope to others. It has been an exciting journey. While we never know what is around the corner in life, we can miss out on a lot of joy by not venturing there. I like the way the prophet Isaiah put it: "*Forget the former things; do not dwell on the past. See, I am doing a new thing! Now it springs up; do you not perceive it? I am making a way in the wilderness and streams in the wasteland*" (Isaiah 43:18–20). Yes, God wants to do new and exciting things in our lives, but we must be willing to be open to them and willing to move on. My life is a testimony to that!

### Moving On in a Spirit of Joy

It's sad—oh so sad—that many people who profess to be followers of our Lord allow themselves to get bogged down under the circumstances of life and then show forth a glum, lugubrious spirit instead of the spirit of joy that is a "*fruit of the Spirit*" (Galatians 5:22). It's one thing to decide to move on from a painful experience but another to decide the spirit in which we will accomplish that. We

---

[4] C. S. Lewis, quoted on Goodreads, http://www.goodreads.com/quotes/6779616-getting-over-a-painful-experience-is-much-like-crossing-monkey.

can adopt a gritting-our-teeth spirit, or we can make a decision to move on in a spirit of joy. The choice is ours.

The apostle Paul had learned to live in a spirit of joy and with a song on his lips, even when in a prison cell in Philippi for preaching the gospel (Acts 16:25). Yes, in the middle of the night, he and his associate Silas broke out in perhaps one of the most amazing duets ever sung, and without instrumental accompaniment. Talk about adapting to the circumstances! No instrument available? Sing a cappella, like many Mennonites do at every meeting. I wonder what the words of the song were. Perhaps they sang Psalm 27:1 (*"The LORD is my light and my salvation—whom shall I fear?"*) or Psalm 34:1 (*"I will extol the LORD at all times; his praise will always be on my lips"*).

I thank God that as I have moved on in my life from each trauma, I have been able to do so with a song of praise on my lips. I am blessed to have stored in my memory bank the words and tunes of hundreds of Christian hymns, and I sing, hum or whistle them all day long, from the moment I awake until I fall asleep at night. Yes, indeed, *"His praise will always be on my lips"* (Psalm 34:1). I encourage you to try it; you might get to like it!

Chapter 2
# TRAUMAS RELIEVED THROUGH SEVEN PILLARS

## PILLAR 1: A STRONG FAITH

I have shared in chapter 1 the three principles that have enabled me to deal in a positive manner with the traumas I have experienced in my life, and now I share the seven pillars upon which I have also built my life, which enabled me to face my traumas with a smile on my face, a sparkle in my eyes, a spring in my step and a song (or whistle) on my lips. I have used the adjective "strong" purposely as it describes perfectly my faith: "Very confident and able to deal with difficult situations" (*Merriam Webster Learning Dictionary*). That is how the Psalmist felt when he wrote, "*Clap your hands, all you nations; shout to God with cries of joy. For the LORD Most High is awesome, the great King over all the earth*" (Psalm 47:1–2). And also "*I will extol the LORD at all times; his praise will always be on my lips*" (Psalm 34:1, emphasis added). It's no wonder with a faith like that, that I sing or whistle or hum the praises of God from when I wake up in the morning until I pillow my head at night! Hallelujah!

### Seeing Is Believing

The apostle Paul wrote to one of his proteges, a young pastor by the name of Timothy, "*From childhood you have known the Holy Scriptures*" (2 Timothy 3:15, NKJV) and "*I am reminded of your sincere faith, which first lived in your grandmother Lois and in your mother Eunice*" (2 Timothy 1:5).

How blessed I was to see faith in action in the everyday life of my mother! Mom was born and brought up in Bristol, England, and when she was in her early twenties, she was doing domestic work (cleaning homes) and also volunteering at a soldiers' hospital that housed men returning from the First World War who had been injured on the battlefield. One of these soldiers was my dad, born in Oslo, Norway, where he had learned the tool and die trade in his dad's and uncle's company. In his early thirties he immigrated to Montreal, and when the First

World War broke out in 1914 he joined the Canadian army, in the Fourteenth Battalion, and was shipped overseas. Where he served, we do not know, as he would never talk about his war experience, which is customary for many soldiers returning from the bloody battlefields of war. What we do know is that shrapnel entered his cranium, and it was decided that removing it would probably end his life, so he lived with it lodged in his head for the rest of his life. How much this contributed to his psychological problems, we will never know. Could it be that my dad had what we now call PTSD (post-traumatic stress disorder)? Another contributing factor to his psychological problems could have been the death of his younger brother at six years of age within a few days of becoming ill. According to his older sister he loved his little brother dearly, and she felt that his death left my dad feeling very bitter. We know that a "spirit of bitterness" seemed to permeate every aspect of my dad's life and resulted in our home often being a place of dreadful and frightful unrest.

This unrest put a very heavy burden on my beloved mom, who did everything in her power to keep our home as pleasant a place as possible. Yes, indeed, we witnessed every day my mom's strong faith come shining through the darkness of the unrest, and it resulted in us having lots of happy and light times in our home. Mom loved to play table games with us all and to entertain us with her wonderful sense of humour. Mom's example of a Christian life resulted in all ten of us children walking in the footsteps of her walk with God and living fruitful lives with a strong and vibrant faith. We also all had lots of good friends at school, in the community and at church. Church was such an important part of our growing up—attending services twice on Sundays, plus Sunday school and weekday youth group—and we all had lots of diversions that we were involved in, including many kinds of sporting activities.

Mom's strong faith kept her living in a light spirit that was evidenced by her singing hymns all day long. Her favourite hymn, which we heard her sing often around our home, was "What a Friend We Have in Jesus."

### Loss of Sleep and Loss of My Dad

We didn't know from one night to the next if we were going to get a good night's sleep, and we couldn't invite friends into our home because we never knew when my dad would get into one of his violent temper tantrums. It was an extremely painful time for those of us who were still at home. Four of my sisters by this time had married, and that left four sisters still at home along with my brother and me. My dad's behaviour reached the point where it simply could not be tolerated any longer, certainly not if we were to get the sleep we all needed.

So as the eldest of the two boys, the responsibility of taking action fell upon my shoulders. It was a heavy one to bear for a teenager. However I have never been afraid to move ahead when I felt in my heart it was the right thing to do and that God would be with me. Looking back now some 70 years later, I realize that I was beginning to formulate in my mind the three principles and seven pillars that I have built my life on that enabled me to face the multiple traumas of my life without buckling under.

In my teens I was blessed to have a wonderful pastor and a Bible class teacher whose teachings and lives—along with my mom's as stated—were very instrumental in helping me develop a strong and vibrant faith. I memorized many passages of Scripture that to this day I can recall and that keep me strong in my faith, passages such as "*Underneath are the everlasting arms*" (Deuteronomy 33:27); "*Even youths grow tired and weary, and young men stumble and fall; but those who hope in the* LORD *will renew their strength. They will soar on wings like eagles; they will run and not grow weary, they will walk and not be faint*" (Isaiah 40:30–31); "*Do not fear, for I am with you; do not be dismayed, for I am your God. I will strengthen you and help you; I will uphold you with my righteous right hand*" (Isaiah 41:10); "*When you pass through the waters, I will be with you*" (Isaiah 43:2); and "*I can do all things through Christ who strengthens me*" (Philippians 4:13, NKJV).

## So What?

Someone might say "So you have a strong faith—so what?" It has meant to me, through all my traumas, a sense of God's presence and peace.

We have all known people in whose presence we feel joyful and at peace. The Psalmist said, "*In Your presence is fullness of joy*" (Psalm 16:11, NKJV). To the people of Israel God said, "*My Presence will go with you, and I will give you rest*" (Exodus 33:14). I have found fullness of joy and rest in that presence!

When my boys were young, from time to time they would wake up during the night and, feeling afraid, cry out, "Daddy!" I would rush into their room, give them a hug, and in a soft but reassuring voice say, as I called them by name, "Daddy's here." With that assurance they would go back to sleep. That's the kind of security and rest we can have when we experience the presence of God in our lives, whatever may be going on. God's presence and peace can calm any troubled waters we may go through, no matter how stormy they may become.

The prophet Isaiah wrote, "*When you pass through the waters, I will be with you; and when you pass through the rivers, they will not sweep over you*" (Isaiah 43:2). He was saying that because of a sense of God's presence in our lives, we don't have to feel overwhelmed or overcome by anything that comes our way.

When the apostle Paul was sailing for Rome in the midst of a violent storm (so violent that everyone on board gave up hope of being saved), he stood up and shouted out, "*Last night an angel of the God to whom I belong and whom I serve stood beside me and said, 'Do not be afraid, Paul*'" (Acts 27:23–24). That's the voice we *need* to hear and *will* hear (by faith) in the midst of our storms of life.

The 23rd psalm has probably been read at funeral services more often than any other passage of the Bible. The Psalmist was more realistic than many people I know and was not reluctant or afraid to talk about his death in a very personal way. He said (and I paraphrase), "Yes, I know I am going to have to go through the dark valley of death, but when I do I will not be afraid, because I know the Good Shepherd will be with me" (see verse 4). Ah, that has brightened up every dark valley I have been through and will those I have yet to go through.

When God commanded Moses to go tell Pharaoh to release the people of God, Moses reneged and said, "Lord, I'm not up to carrying out that task!" God could have pushed back on that excuse and tried to reason with Moses, but He didn't. He said, "Moses, I am going to go with you" (see Exodus 3). With that sense of assurance, Moses fulfilled the task God had assigned to him. When Moses was handing over the reins to his successor, he gave this message to Joshua: "*Do not be afraid...for the LORD your God goes with you; he will never leave you nor forsake you*" (Deuteronomy 31:6). We all know the experience of having that special person with us when we are going through a dark valley of life. It was what our Lord meant when He said, "*I am with you always*" (Matthew 28:20).

In prophesying the birth of Jesus, Isaiah declared that the baby would be called "*Immanuel*" (Isaiah 7:14), which means "God is with us." Practice His presence in your life today and you will experience "*the peace of God, which transcends all understanding*" (Philippians 4:7).

### Good-News Ending!

I thank God that the part of the story to do with my dad has a good-news ending. While I was living away from our home, my dad had a heart attack and was taken to the soldiers' wing of Sunnybrook Hospital in Toronto. One day a nurse called me and said that my dad wanted to see me. I boarded two streetcars and a bus to get there, but it was a journey well worthwhile. When I walked into my dad's room I reached out and gave him a big hug. He looked up at me, and we smiled at each other. What a glorious memory to have in my memory bank! I said, "Dad, I'm going to pray with you that everything will be right between you and me and between you and God."

He said, "Yes, I want that."

I believe that my dad made his peace with God at that moment and someday I will see him and embrace him again. Someday he will be part of the Nullmeyer family circle in heaven when all 12 of us embrace one another and thank God for His love and mercy that reached out to each one of us, including my dad in his final days. I gave him one more hug and left his room, weeping buckets but now buckets of joy that my dad and I and my dad and his God were at peace. In two days I received a call saying that my dad had passed away. Yes—I believe—passed into the very presence of our Lord Jesus. Glory to God!

Our family was all in attendance at Dad's funeral service, and we celebrated his strengths, which were many. We always knew he loved us all, and during the Great Depression (with 12 of us to support) he was willing to work at anything that came along, which was not easy for a proud and accomplished tool and die maker. I personally benefited greatly from the gifts he passed on to me, having a sharp eye for details (basic to being a tool and die maker) and being able to do so many things with my hands.

### More than Triumphant!

Yes, it is my strong and vibrant faith that has gotten me through everything that has been thrown at me in life, and not just through but with a triumphant spirit, as the apostle Paul speaks of in Romans 8:37: "*In all these things we are more than conquerors through him who loved us.*" This triumphant spirit has enabled me to keep a smile on my face, a sparkle in my eyes, a spring in my step and a song on my lips, and all because I have learned that "*I can do all things through Christ who strengthens me*" (Philippians 4:13, NKJV).

### Praising My Saviour All the Day Long!

The good news is that this strength is available to anyone and everyone who will put their trust in Christ and walk in His ways. My daily walk in the Lord can be summarized in two seven-word statements, "All the way my Saviour leads me" and "Praising my Saviour all the day long," lines from hymns written by Fanny J. Crosby.

## PILLAR 2: A LIGHT SPIRIT
Nully Nugget: "A light spirit will see us through the dark and heavy times of life."

### Like Mom, Like Son
As the strong and vibrant faith I have is a result of seeing it in action through my mom, so also is my light spirit from that source. In the previous chapter I described how my mom's life was anything but easy. However, in spite of that, she never did lose her light spirit. I can still remember returning home from school or elsewhere and hearing my mom either singing or humming one of her many favourite hymns. One of these was "What a Friend We Have in Jesus." There's a proverb in the Bible that perfectly describes my mom: "*Strength and dignity are her clothing. She laughs at the time to come*" (Proverbs 31:25, WEB).

### Blessings Others with Our Light Spirit
When I am out and about and whistling or humming one of my favourite hymns, often someone will say, "You sound happy." But even when I am not feeling super-happy, I whistle anyway, as it lightens my spirit. One of my daily goals when I'm out shopping or in the coffee shop is to make people laugh. Recently while checking out my groceries, I noticed that the cashier looked sad and troubled, so I thought maybe I'd try to lighten her up. So I started in (there was no lineup behind me) and got her really laughing. I said to her, "You look prettier when you laugh." As she continued checking me out she gave me a lovely smile, and as I was walking away she said, "Sir, thank you; you have made my day." The woman who owns the coffee shop nearby says every time I walk through the door, "Oh, Ernie, I like it when you come in; you make me feel happy. You lift me up!" And why is that? Well, part of it could be the tip I often leave, but more, I believe, it's because I get her laughing.

One of my Nully Nuggets says, "Life is too short to take it too seriously" and another says, "A light spirit will see us through the dark and heavy times of life." To be sure (as I have written about in part 1) we are all going to have dark and heavy days, but none of them cannot be lightened a little through a light spirit. So I encourage you today to lighten up. Not only will you feel better, but you will make everyone around you feel better.

### Time to Lighten Up
I am saddened when I walk through a department store and see most people looking so heavy and burdened down. Have they all recently been through such a

bad time that it makes them look so lugubrious? That word comes from the Latin *legere*, which means "to be mournful." Sometimes I feel like getting on the public address system and shouting out, "Lighten up, everyone! We live in the best country in the world." Yes, the Bible does say there is "*a time to weep and…a time to mourn*," but the verse also says there is "*a time to laugh…and a time to dance*" (Ecclesiastes 3:4). (Even Baptists are allowed that kind of dancing—praise God!)

### The Best Prescription
The Bible has it right when it says, "*A merry heart does good, like medicine*" (Proverbs 17:22, NKJV). Perhaps then the best prescription physicians could hand out to their patients would be to give them something to laugh about before they leave the office. That's why I wrote this Nully Nugget: "Laughter …the best medicine…no prescription required…no overdosing possible!" The proverb goes on to say, "*But a broken spirit dries the bones.*" Notice the connection of the spirit and the physical. So if you want to feel better, lighten up and laugh often and loudly!

### Getting the Diagnosis Right
On a visit I made to my family physician, she started out by saying, "I enjoy your visits because you always give me a good laugh." I told her the story of the young doctors who were attending a conference on "Getting the Diagnosis Correct." As they were walking along the street looking for a place to have lunch they noticed a man up ahead who was limping very badly. One said to the others, "I wonder what his problem is." "Oh," said one, "obviously he has spinal stenosis." Another said, "No, it's obvious he needs surgery for his hernia." The third doctor said, "Neither of you has it right; his problem is he needs hip surgery." "Well," he continued, "let's catch up to him and find out." They did, explaining the situation to him and relating their various diagnoses. His response: "It's that tailor of mine; he always cuts my pants too tight."

### Seniors Need to Lighten Up
Recently I was at a seniors' luncheon. As the theme was "Celebrating Valentines," a male quartet sang upbeat songs about love. I looked around at the 75 or so seniors present, and only three of us were smiling and getting into the beat and looked like we were having a good time. I thought to myself, *They're passing up a great opportunity to lighten up and allow their spirits to get caught up in the beat of the music and at the same time relax their muscles, which is always good for one's health.*

One of the first things I do every morning—before I prepare my breakfast—is to turn on the TV to the "Light and Easy" music channel. I then often find myself dancing around the room to the beat of the music and smiling broadly while I do (breakfast can wait). Wow! What a great kick-off to the day! And what a great muscle relaxer!

## Learning from Little Children

Isn't it amazing that when we see little children in war-torn countries, they are still smiling and laughing and dancing around? So, if them, why not us? If someday you are really feeling down, walk through a department store or mall just for the purpose of beholding the children. One or two may be unhappy for the moment because they didn't get their way about something, but most of them will be dancing and laughing and living it up. It is sad that so many people lose their childhood spirit so soon in life. They allow the burdens of life (and there are many!) to weigh them down and take control so there is no lightness in their spirit. I recently attended a kindergarten open house to be with my six-year-old twin granddaughters. Wow! What an experience! The room was alive with the sound of excited children showing their parents and grandparents their work. Oh, that we could all reignite some of that spirit of excitement and just be childlike again! Today, allow yourself the joy of getting excited about those little blessings of life that you so often just take for granted.

## The Daily News in Small Doses

Let me insert here a warning about getting too caught up in the news of the world. Yes, there is nothing wrong about knowing what is going on in the world, but do not allow your spirit to get too caught up with all the bad news. It will drag you down! The *Globe and Mail* used to have a feature called "A Lighter Moment" in which they related a joke. It provided a little comic relief from the heaviness of the news written about throughout the paper. It was the best part.

One of the reasons I watch a certain news program is because they often feature some light item, which is often a good-news story that highlights a group or individual that's making a difference in our world. It is presented by a reporter whose very smile and enthusiasm will bring a smile to your face and lighten up your life. I wish every newscast would conclude with some little item that would leave listeners feeling up instead of down.

## The Bible and Joy

The Bible has much to say on the subject of joy and gladness or, as I call it, lightness of spirit. That is why I have always found it strange that many who profess to be followers of Jesus don't express any joy or enthusiasm about it and don't want any lightness in a worship service. Some of the same people (I have noticed) can get all excited (as I do, I will confess) when there is a grand slam in a baseball game or a sudden-death goal in a hockey game but can't get excited about the things of God or about the amazing grace that John Newton experienced in his life and then wrote about in the world's best-known hymn.

When I commenced my pastoral ministry I had to make a decision. How much would I allow my light- and joy-filled spirit to enter into the way I conducted worship services, weddings and funerals and many other public engagements? What principles should I be guided by? I decided on the following:

1. I was ordained to be a preacher and teacher of the Word of God, not an entertainer.
2. I would use humour in my homilies but always in keeping with the theme of the sermon. When I was preaching on the tough subject of giving I could use an illustration my pastor used back when I was a youth. A mother gave her son two nickels, saying, "Now, Johnny, one of those is for God, and you are to place it on the Sunday school offering plate; the other you can keep and buy candy with on Monday." (All stores back then were closed on Sundays.) While Johnny was running off to Sunday school one of the nickels fell out of his hand and rolled down the sewer. Johnny looked up to heaven and said, "Well, God, I'm sorry to have to tell You this, but there goes Your nickel."
3. I wanted my listeners to walk out after the service feeling more up, more inspired, more light-spirited, and more joyful than when they walked in.

I felt that I couldn't go wrong if I followed the example of the prophet Isaiah:

*The spirit of the Sovereign LORD is on me, because the LORD has anointed me to proclaim good news to the poor. He has sent me to bind up the brokenhearted…to comfort to all who mourn, and provide for those who grieve in Zion—to bestow on them a crown of beauty instead of ashes, the oil of joy instead of mourning, and a garment of praise instead of a spirit of despair.* (Isaiah 61:1–3)

That should be the modus operandi of every preacher who preaches the gospel, which literally means "good news."

## Lightening Up Sermons

Perhaps the greatest blessing I imparted to my congregants when they were listening (I hope they were!) to the theological truths I was seeking to impart was when I lightened their spirits and gave them something to laugh about! One of my congregants was a fine young man who was borderline challenged.

Mike loved to laugh, and every Sunday as I was shaking hands on the way out, Mike would say, "Oh, Pastor Ernie, you are so funny; I love your jokes." It may not have said much about my well-prepared theological treatise, but it made his day. As I have listened to preachers, I have often felt like standing up and saying, "Lighten it up, my brother; these dear listeners are all carrying heavy burdens, and what they need is a good, hearty laugh! Give them a good dose of the best medicine" (see Proverbs 17:22).

## Lightening Up Congregational Singing

Worship services in many churches have changed dramatically from when I was in my youth and during the years of my pastoral ministry. There is much less formality in many church services now, including the way people dress. Hand-clapping, hand-raising, and praise and worship bands are now featured in many church services, although bands have been an integral part of the Salvation Army services since its founding in 1865. It is also true that God's chosen people—the Israelites—clapped their hands and raised their hands when in a spirit of worship (Psalm 47:1, 98:8; Isaiah 55:12).

The new style of worship has certainly raised the ire of many churchgoing people, even causing divisions within some churches, and raises the question, which style does God prefer? Perhaps the real question should be, does God really care, as long as the individual's worship is genuine and glorifies Him? Two principles from God's Word are apropos here:

1. "*The LORD looks at the heart*" (1 Samuel 16:7; see also 2 Chronicles 6:30). A minister was asked how many worshippers he had in attendance on Sunday. He responded, "I have no idea. I know we had about 500 people in attendance, but only God knows if they were worshipping."
2. True worship must come from a pure heart. "*Who may ascend into the hill of the LORD? Or who may stand in His holy place? He who has clean hands and a pure heart, Who has not lifted up his soul to an idol, Nor sworn deceitfully*" (Psalm 24:3–4, NKJV).

These truths should lead us to believe that what we wear to church and what style the worship service follows are not important to God! Therefore we should attend a church where our personality best fits in and then refrain from criticizing other Christians who choose to attend a service that best fits their personality.

The prophet Isaiah equated joy with being redeemed. He declared,

*"This is what the LORD says—Israel's King and Redeemer, the LORD Almighty...Israel, I will not forget you. I have swept away your offenses like a cloud, and your sins like the morning mist. Return to me, for I have redeemed you." Sing for joy, you heavens, for the LORD has*

*done this; shout aloud, you earth beneath. Burst into song, you mountains, you forests and all your trees, for the LORD has redeemed Jacob, he displays his glory in Israel.* (Isaiah 44:6–23)

Wow!

## The Psalmists Got It Right

Christians and Jews alike love the Psalms. They are songs that express how the writer is feeling in his heart, including sadness—*"I am worn out from groaning. All night long I flood my bed with weeping and drench my couch with tears"* (Psalm 6:6), anger—*"I envied the arrogant when I saw the prosperity of the wicked. They have no struggles; their bodies are healthy and strong. They are free from common human burdens"* (Psalm 73:3–5), and gladness—*"For in the day of trouble…I will sacrifice with shouts of joy; I will sing and make music to the LORD"* (Psalm 27:5–6), *"You make known to me the path of life; you will fill me with joy in your presence"* (Psalm 16:11), *"Clap your hands, all you nations; shout to God with cries of joy. For the LORD Most High is awesome"* (Psalm 47:1–2), *"My lips will shout for joy when I sing praise to you—I whom you have delivered"* (Psalm 71:23), *"For you make me glad by your deeds, LORD; I sing for joy at what your hands have done"* (Psalm 92:4), and *"Our mouths were filled with laughter, our tongues with songs of joy. Then it was said among the nations, 'The LORD has done great things for them.' The LORD has done great things for us, and we are filled with joy"* (Psalm 126:2–3).

For a fuller treatment of this subject see appendix 3, "Praise and Worship."

## The Early Church and Worship

The first worship service of the early church must have been something else to be part of. The Scripture record says,

> When the day of Pentecost came, they were all together in one place. Suddenly a sound *[probably some would have called it "noise"]* like the blowing of a violent wind came from heaven and filled the whole house where they were sitting. They saw what seemed to be tongues of fire that separated and came to rest on each of them. All of them were filled with the Holy Spirit and began to speak in other tongues as the Spirit enabled them. (Acts 2:1–4)

That was no quiet, dignified, liturgical worship service, and all of it was planned and carried out by the Holy Spirit. Imagine being in a worship service like that! I wonder how many walked out in disgust and protest against the change in the order of service and not doing worship the way it had always been. Uh! Huh!

## An Exciting Worship Service

To many churchgoers that may sound like an oxymoron—but it isn't! During the process of rebuilding the wall of the city of Jerusalem, Ezra the scribe, Nehemiah the governor and the Levites (priests) gathered the people of God together to read from the book of the Law of God and to lead in a praise meeting. When Ezra began to praise the Lord for all His goodness, the people all raised their hands to God in corporate praise, shouting "Amen and Amen!" Nehemiah then instructed the congregation to go and live it up with choice foods and sweet drinks (wine, even). He also instructed them to share their goodies with those who hadn't prepared anything. He admonished them to stop their grieving and reminded them that *"the joy of the LORD is your strength"* (Nehemiah 8:10).

I can just hear some people of faith reacting to all that display of excitement with comments like "My goodness, the impertinence of people having a good time at a worship service! This must stop, as it's not the way we've always done it around here!" "Let's not get carried away with this emotional stuff, and I don't go for this showing emotion when it comes to expressing religion." Or "I don't think clapping and that kind of thing has any place in a worship service." Sad!

When the ark of the covenant was brought back to the temple, God's people held a celebration that they would never forget (2 Chronicles 5). The Levites (priests who were professional musicians) dressed up in fine linen and played cymbals (a concave brass plate struck with a stick to make loud and clashing sounds), harps and lyres (a small harp with a sound box made from a turtle shell with strings attached). These musicians were joined by 120 priests playing trumpets and a mighty chorus of singers. Wow! What a sound! What a celebration! What a worship service! It reminds me of that great day that the apostle John tried his best to describe for us in the book of Revelation when he heard what *"sounded like the roar of a great multitude in heaven shouting: 'Hallelujah!...' And again they shouted 'Hallelujah!...Praise our God...For our Lord God Almighty reigns. Let us rejoice and be glad and give him glory!'"* (Revelation 19:1–7).

## Jesus and Joy

So that was then, but what about now? Has our Lord called us to live in a spirit of joy? Here is what the record says in answer to that question. In our Lord's high priestly prayer (John 15–17), which came at the conclusion of the Last Supper as He was anticipating going to the Cross, three times Jesus spoke of what His life and death were all about: *joy*! (John 15:11, 16:24, 17:13). And joy that was full and complete! Jesus didn't promise His followers happiness, because that depends on happenings, which come and go, but rather joy, which is *not* affected by what is happening in our lives.

## The Apostle Paul and Joy

In his letter to his fellow believers at Thessalonica the apostle Paul picked up on our Lord's promise to give His followers joy: "*Rejoice always*" (1 Thessalonians 5:16). Paul continued this theme of joy in his letter to the believers at Philippi. In spite of the fact that he was in prison for preaching the gospel, he highlighted the theme of living in a spirit of joy under all circumstances. Was he happy to be in prison? Of course not! But he was joyous in the Lord because he knew that whatever circumstance he might be in, he could enjoy the presence and peace of God. He wrote of joy and rejoicing in all four chapters of the book (a total of ten times) and culminated with that glorious and triumphant admonition to "*Rejoice in the Lord always. Again I will say, rejoice!*" (Philippians 4:4, NKJV). Wow! In all of literature there is no more profound statement that states without equivocation the difference between being happy and being joyous.

Am I happy about all the traumas I have experienced in life? Of course not! But God has enabled me to get through them all with a light spirit, a spirit of rejoicing in every circumstance of life! That's why I can have a smile on my face, a sparkle in my eyes, a spring in my step, and a song (or whistle) on my lips. To God be the glory; great things He has done!

## The Apostle Peter and Joy

The apostle Peter wrote, "*Though you have not seen him, you love him; and even though you do not see him now, you believe in him and are filled with an inexpressible and glorious joy*" (1 Peter 1:8), a joy so glorious, says Peter, that we just can't put it into words. That's the spirit of joy that ought to characterize our lives every moment of every day, whatever may be *happening* in our lives.

We're all familiar with the expression "getting off on the right foot." That is what needs to happen if we are to live out the day in a light spirit and a spirit of joy. The moment I wake up (and before I get my feet on the floor) I start humming a happy tune (usually one of the hundreds of hymns that I have known since my youth and have stored in my memory bank), hymns like "There Is Sunshine in My Soul Today" and "Cheer Up Ye Saints of God":

Cheer up ye saints of God
There's nothing to worry about
Nothing to make you feel afraid
Nothing to make you doubt

Remember Jesus never fails
So why not trust Him and shout
You'll be sorry you worried at all
Tomorrow morning

## Living with Joyous Enthusiasm

"Enthusiasm"—the very word seems to conjure up a feeling of excitement. Synonyms are "eager enjoyment," "fervour," "passion" and "zeal." Allow me to ask you, when was the last time you had one of those feelings? It ought to be a daily experience, even many times throughout the day. Without enthusiasm in our daily living, life becomes boring, humdrum and tiresome. Yes, tiresome! An absence of enthusiasm in our spirit will lead to physical fatigue and lethargy. The biblical proverb says just that: *"A cheerful [enthusiastic] heart is good medicine, but a crushed [unenthusiastic] spirit dries up the bones"* (Proverbs 17:22).

The moment we experience enthusiasm about something, we will feel the effect of it physically—and mentally! How often when we feel too tired to take in some event, we discover that when we make a decision to do so, it makes a world of difference in our energy level.

Observe children in the schoolyard at recess (as I often do around the corner from my condo) and note their boundless energy. Where's that coming from? It's coming from their uninhibited, enthusiastic spirits. Henry David Thoreau wrote, "None are so old as those who have outlived enthusiasm."[5]

I struck up a conversation with an elderly man in a coffee shop. I asked him if he was still living on his own. "Oh yes," he said with enthusiasm, "my wife and I bought the little house over 50 years ago. We always talked about getting the old kitchen renovated but never did get around to it. She is deceased now, so I decided to go ahead and renovate the kitchen, and I am really excited to see how it will look."

We equate maturity (getting older) with settling down and not enjoying life anymore. That is so sad and so unnecessary! Believe me, my days are filled with things to be enthusiastic about. You might ask, "What is your secret to living in a spirit of enthusiasm at your age?" The answer is simple and found in two words: *think small!* I know that the advice we usually receive about living a fulfilled life is to *think big!* And that is usually good advice, but not when it comes to practising a gratitude-attitude (part 2, chapter 3) or living in a spirit of enthusiasm.

---

[5] Henry David Thoreau, Brainy Quote, https://www.brainyquote.com/quotes/quotes/h/henrydavid103923.html.

## Enthusiasm About Small Blessings

If we feel enthusiasm only about the big things that happen in our lives, the experience will be rare; but when we think small there is no limit to how often we can feel enthusiasm coursing through our emotional veins. Little things like

- a brilliant blue sky
- an amazing cloud formation
- the happy song of a bird
- children at play
- coffee with a friend
- a table game
- a good book
- fresh fruit
- a bouquet of flowers
- a bowl of delicious homemade soup
- a visit from a grandchild or great-grandchild
- a glass of uncontaminated water (think First Nations reserves)
- a breath of pure air (an exception in many countries)
- a glorious sunset
- a seniors' luncheon

When we went to Florida each winter we loved to join with the crowds at the beach at sunset. Thousands of people—of all ages—would line up along the seawall waiting for the setting of the sun, and the moment the big red ball dipped below the horizon, everyone would shout out as if they had all just won the multimillion-dollar lottery. Only you didn't need to buy a ticket for this exciting event!

## In a Wheelchair, But...

While others were looking grumpy at having to wait in the long lineup for their order in the fast food outlet, one little fellow filled the air with his happy sounds, waiting for his Happy Meal number to be called out. You might ask, "What's so significant about that?" Well, nothing, until you know that he was confined to a wheelchair, where he will be spending the rest of his life. This little fellow had learned what many adults have never learned—to enjoy enthusiastically the little blessings of life! Have you learned that? Have I learned that? It's not too late to get started. How about today?

There are so many things—throughout every day—to feel enthusiastic about, but we must open the eyes of our spirit to see them and to experience them on a daily basis. Allow yourself to think small, and enjoy the difference that a little enthusiasm can make in your life today and every day henceforth!

Someone has said, "Enthusiasm, like measles and the common cold, is contagious—except in a good way." Many people have come into my life and instantly blessed me (and many others) with their enthusiasm. One of these is my beloved soulmate Carolyn, whose enthusiasm for life I have written about in part 1, chapter 6.

Another is Carolyn's mom, Jean Lois Cameron. From early morning to bedtime, she lived out Ecclesiastes 9:10: "*Whatever your hand finds to do, do it with all your might [with enthusiasm].*" When she was out working in her very large garden (most of it to bless others with), she did so with enthusiasm. I remember the day when Carolyn and I were helping her harvest her potato crop. She was right into it with enthusiasm, even though she was in her late eighties. She would say, "Oh, look at this one; it's a beauty!" Imagine getting enthused about a potato; now that's thinking small! It's no wonder that her husband—an enthusiastic person and farmer in his own right—believed (and said often) that Jean was the best wife a man could have. No wonder also that the Cameron farming operation was such a success, with two people like Don and Jean doing their work ("chores") all those years with enthusiasm!

It was such a joy to arrive when Jean was preparing dinner for a large number. She did it with enthusiasm. When working on her quilts or hooked rugs or baking her delicious pies or her scrumptious bread, she did it all with enthusiasm! It's no wonder she was still working on those projects until she took ill with the cancer that ended her earthly journey in her early nineties.

## A Model of Enthusiasm

When I think of people who blessed others with their enthusiastic spirit, Bessie Smith comes to mind. She was very short in physical stature but had grown into a spiritual giant. She told me about some of the hardships of her life while growing up. These included being born into a totally dysfunctional home, with her parents eventually divorcing and placing her in a foster home—the first of many. She also had a baby out of wedlock with a teenager who flew the coop when informed that she was pregnant. Experiencing the stigma of living on social assistance—and determined that she would get off it as soon as possible—Bessie started her own little housecleaning business. Because of her enthusiasm to do a good job, she soon was able to choose whom she would work for. One Sunday she decided to go to church, and because our church was just around the corner from where she lived, she turned up in ours. After she had listened many times to the message of the gospel, Bessie made a decision to commit her life to Christ.

She became one of the most enthusiastic Christians I have ever known. One day, while out doing house calls, I decided to visit Bessie. As she opened the door, all of a sudden I felt like royalty as I was greeted with one of the most enthusiastic welcomes I had ever had in all my pastoral visits. As I looked around at the furniture and furnishings I thought to myself that it all looked like it should be on the way to a Goodwill store. And then—with a burst of enthusiasm—Bessie said, "Oh, Pastor! Hasn't God been good to me, giving me all this beautiful furniture?"

I realized that I was in the presence of someone who had learned Paul the Apostle's secret: "*I have learned to be content whatever the circumstances*" (Philippians 4:11). But Bessie took it one step further, being not only content but enthusiastic about what she had in life, even though it was relatively so little. Bessie had also learned what our Lord taught us: "*Life does not consist in an abundance of possessions*" (Luke 12:15), as well as "*If riches increase, Do not set your heart on them*" (Psalm 62:10, NKJV). We all need to pay attention to these principles about material possessions.

"Hold earthly possessions with hands open to God's guidance."

"You have never seen a U-Haul on the back of a hearse."

"God doesn't condemn us for having earthly possessions, as long as they don't have us!"

After a few minutes of fellowshipping together, Bessie said to me, "Oh, Pastor, I would like to serve you tea; have you got time for that?" Well, if I had to cancel all other engagements for the day I was not going to miss out on that blessing! The teapot was not a Limoges, and neither were the cups and saucers, but the fellowship was rich, warm and uplifting. Of course we had a prayer of thanks before we partook, and Bessie had to add a word: "Oh, Pastor, what a beautiful prayer! This is so wonderful to be having tea with my pastor." Now that's enthusiasm personified!

Let me hasten to say that I have nothing against fine china, as Carolyn and I had some of it ourselves (before we downsized and donated it to a thrift store to bless others). On numerous occasions I have enjoyed dinner served on very fine expensive china, and it was served with a warm and loving heart.

## Prayer Time with Bessie

Before I left, I read a Psalm and had prayer with Bessie. When I said, "Amen," Bessie said, "Oh, Pastor, I would like to pray for you." She prayed as beautiful and rich a prayer as I have ever heard uttered, thanking God for "sending us this fine young man" and praying that God would "bless him in all his labours of love." I dropped in to be a blessing to Bessie, but I left being blessed by her, an enthusiastic follower of Jesus.

### Enthusiastic Even in a Nursing Home

As Bessie approached her ninetieth birthday, we made arrangements for her to be admitted to a nursing home, where with her inimitable enthusiasm she immediately became a blessing to staff and residents. I visited her often (to bless her and to receive a blessing). Bessie went to be with her Lord and Saviour in her sleep, and I had the honour of officiating at her service of celebration. We celebrated the life of a lady who was small in physical stature but a spiritual giant, the epitome of an enthusiastic Christian. Heaven will be richer because Bessie Smith will be there!

As I close this chapter, allow me to remind you again that life is too short to take it too seriously. Allow yourself to get enthusiastic about something, today and every day! You will be a better person for it, and others will be blessed by it.

### PILLAR 3: A GRATITUDE-ATTITUDE

I am blessed to have witnessed the gratitude-attitude in the life of my mom. Even though there were lots of bad things in her life she could have complained about, she never allowed them to cloud over the good things she could be grateful for. Mom had learned that the key to having a gratitude-attitude is to count our blessings one by one. This is expressed in a hymn she sang often while going about her daily domestic duties, a hymn written by Johnson Oatman Jr., entitled "Count Your Blessings."

> When upon life's billows you are tempest-tossed
> When you are discouraged, thinking all is lost,
> Count your many blessings, name them one by one,
> And it will surprise you what the Lord has done.

### Always Something to Be Grateful for

Through the years of my pastoral ministry I was often called upon to counsel with parishioners who were feeling down about everything in life. It's difficult in that situation to know exactly what to do and say. However, I discovered that the best way (and only way, really) to help bring someone out of the doldrums and their feelings of melancholy was to get them to think of *one* thing for which they could be grateful. It was amazing how well this approach worked. Soon they would rhyme off a whole litany of blessings they could be grateful for.

Another approach is to think of someone who is worse off than we are, which shouldn't be difficult to do. The fact of the matter is that, no matter how many tough situations we have been through (and many people, through no fault of their own, have had more than their fair share), there are always things to be thankful for.

When I find Carolyn in one of her very low and discouraged moods, all I can do is hold her and whisper into her ear about what a beautiful and absolutely amazing life God has given us together. That always elicits a little smile, which in turn brightens me up also.

One evening when I felt too tired to watch TV or read, I took pen and pad in hand and began writing down all the blessings I had enjoyed that day. I was up to over 40 blessings when weariness overtook me and I fell asleep in my Lazy Boy chair. Through the years I have developed a habit of, after climbing into bed, going over one by one the blessings God has so freely bestowed upon me that day. What a way to fall off to sleep and to have a wonderful night's rest and sleep with the words of Johnson Oatman Jr.'s hymn swirling around in my mind: "Count your blessings, name them one by one."

I've thought a lot about why and how some people—and perhaps most people—get into the habit of grumbling and complaining about so many little things that happen in their lives, and I think I have discovered how that happens. I will elucidate my theory and see if you concur with it.

## The Bad Habit of Grumbling

In our childhood years, we develop a habit of complaining and grumbling about all the *little* things that make us unhappy. But then as we leave those childhood years, we don't develop a commensurate habit of expressing gratitude for all the *little* things that make us happy. If the restaurant meal is not to our liking, we will complain about it, but if it's excellent we probably won't express that. If the service is anything but acceptable, we will probably complain, but if it's excellent, will we then express that to the waitress and even leave a generous tip?

## Grumbling People

A spirit of grumbling goes back a long way. When the Israelites were being led by Moses out of the desert to the Promised Land, they got into a grumbling mood and complained that the water was insufficient, the food was insipid, and the leadership was inept. They had lots to thank God for, but their spirit of gratitude got sidelined by a spirit of ingratitude (Exodus 15–17). They made the journey more miserable for themselves and for their fellow travellers.

I'm reminded of a bus tour Carolyn and I took in Scotland. Most of us had a delightful time, but it would have been even more enjoyable without the one lady who complained about absolutely everything. She had not developed a gratitude-attitude (such as being grateful she could afford the tour) and thus made herself a very unhappy lady, one no one wanted to spend any more time with than they had to.

### One Out of Ten
There's a fascinating story in the Bible (Luke 17) of ten men with leprosy who came to Jesus and cried out with a loud voice, "Jesus, Master, have pity on us!" (Luke 17:13). Jesus told them to go and show themselves to the priest, as the priest also practised the healing arts and was the only one who could declare a person with leprosy "clean" if they had indeed been freed of the scourge. As they were on their way to see the priest, the ten men were healed. How many of them do you think would and should have returned to express gratitude to Jesus for healing them? You would think *all* of them, but no—*only one* returned to say thanks. Would you or I be that one, or would we be among the nine? It would all depend whether or not we had developed a *gratitude-attitude*!

### Living in a Spirit of Gratitude
The apostle Paul admonished the believers in Thessalonica to "*Give thanks in all circumstances*" (1 Thessalonians 5:18). He didn't say "give thanks *for* every circumstance," as that would be totally unrealistic. I don't thank God for the major traumas I have had to go through, but I do thank Him that when going through them I have always had a sense of His wonderful grace, presence and peace.

### Teaching the Spirit of Gratitude to Children
If parents want their children to have a gratitude-attitude, they must inculcate that spirit within them as they are growing up. My first wife, Marion, did this when the boys received a money gift from out-of-town aunts and uncles. They were not allowed to have the gift until they wrote a note of thanks. It could be just a few words (which it always was!), but they grew up learning the importance of saying thanks to those who had shown them an act of kindness. A grandmother wrote to an advice columnist, "I need your advice. I keep sending cheques to my

grandchildren for their birthdays, and not *one* of them ever writes back to say thanks. What shall I do?" The columnist wrote back, "Next time, forget to sign the cheque."

## Expressing Gratitude

It's such a blessing to me that my beloved wife Carolyn has always lived with a gratitude-attitude, so that every time I visit with her, she expresses numerous times how much she appreciates all I do for her. In return, I tell her how much I appreciate all that she has meant and done for me through our 40 years of joyful marriage.

## A More Pleasant Way to Live

A gratitude-attitude will make our life's journey so much more pleasant, whatever the circumstances may be, and will also be more pleasant for our family and friends. So today, let each of us determine that we will eliminate the negativity of complaining and start living in the positivity of expressing gratitude for all of the little blessings of life, which for us Canadians are manifold! Let us put off the unbecoming garments of complaining and put on the pulchritudinous garments of gratitude! Let us make a "New Us" resolution (as compared to a New Year's resolution) and declare a day when we will not utter even one complaint! If you have never tried that, you have a treat in store, one that will be a blessing to all the folks you come in contact with that day! "Fill the moments of your days expressing gratitude and there won't be any space left to express grumbling"—a Nully Nugget.

Amen and amen!

## PILLAR 4: A MULTIPLICITY OF DIVERSIONS

The dictionary definition of "diversion" is "something that distracts the mind and relaxes or entertains" (*The Free Dictionary* by Farlex). A synonym is "distraction"—a thing that prevents someone from giving full attention to any one aspect of life. That is why my Nully Nugget says, "Do not live every aspect of your life through the illness of the one you are caring for." If you do (as many have chosen to do), you will not have any life of your own and probably (as statistics show) will predecease the patient you are caring for.

## Heavy Demands on Caregivers

As previously mentioned, the best of many books I have read and studied is *The Memory Clinic: Stories of Hope and Healing for Alzheimer's Patients and*

*Their Families,* by Tiffany Chow, a behavioural neurologist and senior scientist at Baycrest Health Centre in Toronto. The author includes a very meaningful chapter in which she shares some very wise advice for the caregivers of those with Alzheimer's. She writes, "One study concluded that caregivers of patients with dementia were at a higher risk of developing the disease themselves…The demands on the caregiver can last for years. The landscape is always shifting."[6] She then goes on to say how imperative it is for caregivers of a dementia patient to make time for themselves, remembering that while the patient has a caregiver, the caregiver does not! Chow continues to say that dementias can last for as long as 20 years, which is too long to delay gratification of one's own needs. "The primary caregiver of a patient must not live every aspect of their life through the illness of the one they are caring for" (a Nully Nugget).

An article entitled "The Hidden Patient" explores the incredible burden a caregiver of someone with Alzheimer's bears.[7] Most people do not know that a very high percentage of caregivers of Alzheimer patients pass away before the patient they are caring for. (Let me quickly add that I am not planning on that happening to me, and I'm doing everything I can do to prevent it.)

How I thank God that I can still be involved in a multiplicity of diversions to distract me from brooding too much over Carolyn's very heartbreaking decline in health, as Alzheimer's continues to lay an ever stronger hold on her mind and life.

## The Need to Have a Life of Our Own

When I was a resident in a retirement residence, I became involved in almost everything that was on the program, always encouraging others to get involved also. Alas, more often than not without success. I moved out of the retirement residence because I felt—though I was 87—that I needed to be even more active and have more diversions. That's when I moved into a condo, which meant I would be responsible for everything involved in living on one's own. I decided also that I would continue to keep active in a diversity of fun activities: going out for coffee, reading, golfing, going to hockey and baseball games, watching sporting activities on TV, taking in musicals and comedy-dramas, attending seniors luncheons, having lunch with friends, playing hide and seek and other games with my six-year-old twin granddaughters when they come to visit me, and writing the manuscript for this, my new book. I believe that being involved in a multiplicity of diversions has enabled me to be a more relaxed caregiver for

---

[6] Chow, *The Memory Clinic.*

[7] Joal Hill, "The Hidden Patient," *The Lancet,* November 15, 2003, available at http://www. thelancet.com/journals/lancet/article/PIIS0140-6736(03)14820-9/abstract.

my beloved Carolyn. Carolyn is and always has been such a caring person, and often when I visit her she will say to me, "My darling, I hope you are taking care of yourself." So sweet!

## The Need for Fun in Our Lives

As important as it is for a primary caregiver of an ill loved one to be involved in diversions, it is also very important for all seniors. Of course as aging sets in, those fun times will take on a different form, but there are always activities we can get involved in according to our physical and mental abilities. The sad fact is, though, that many seniors give up on every kind of fun activity, and that's a serious mistake. Without fun in our lives we become very dull creatures, so we need to get involved in some activities that will preclude that happening. One of the men at the retirement residence where I lived is in a wheelchair, but he has immersed himself in doing puzzles (not easy ones, either) and enjoys that daily diversion to the full. In fact he whistles the whole time he is putting tiny little pieces together. His finished products are something to behold. A friend of mine in the same facility had to have a leg amputated, but that didn't stop him from having fun. He still gets involved in active games such as bocce ball and shuffleboard, and he does very well. Also, many of the residents are regularly involved in playing cards. That's a great pastime for seniors, and I wish—looking back—that I had learned to play cards. It presents a great opportunity to socialize and have fun together. I had more to say about having fun in life in pillar 2, A Light Spirit.

## Long-Term Care Fun Times

It's difficult for outsiders to believe that there can be any fun times living in a long-term care facility. However, the recreation staff at the LTC where Carolyn is living do an amazing job of creating opportunities for the residents to enjoy life as much as they can. These are highly trained and exceptional people who plan and run recreation activities for the residents. Activities include musical concerts, ice cream cone days, coffee and donut days, sundae days, and games of many kinds geared to the physical and mental levels of the residents. It's a delightful experience to observe the smiles on the faces of the residents as they participate in the activities. In many cases, the staff go around to encourage residents to attend an event and to assist them in getting there. What a wonderful dimension all this adds to the life of a resident in LTC!

## PILLAR 5: A HEALTHY LIFESTYLE

"Ernie Nullmeyer has been a patient in my family practice for seven years. During that time I have observed that Ernie is passionate about practising a healthy lifestyle, which is certainly borne out in the amazing measure of excellent health he has at 88 years of age. Ernie could be the 'poster boy' of a healthy senior.

"In his book, he details what he believes are the principal factors of a healthy lifestyle, which he has put into practice throughout his many years. Readers will do well to give serious attention to those factors and consider applying them to their own life."

Family Physician

In sharing my thoughts about what a healthy lifestyle should look like, I make absolutely no claim to do so as an expert. That kind of advice must be given by those trained in their particular expertise in the medical field.

However, I do believe that sharing what has contributed to my excellent health and abundant energy at 88 years of age might be helpful to others, and if not helpful, then just interesting. Also I need to state that even people who practice a healthy lifestyle—as my beloved Carolyn certainly did—can still become victims of disease, as a bad random act of nature. This was also true of my youngest sister, who passed away at age 49 from cancer, my first wife, at 47 from lupus, and my son, at 52 from a rare virus. However, that should not preclude each of us taking responsibility for our health and living as healthy a lifestyle as possible. What then are the keys that I believe have led to me living a full and healthy life even into my late eighties?

### Key 1: Treat Your Body as a Sacred Gift

In my youth I was taught that—as a follower of the Lord Jesus—my body was a temple and a gift from God, and therefore I had a responsibility to take care of it. *"Do you not know that your body is the temple of the Holy Spirit who is in you, whom you have from God, and you are not your own? For you were bought at a price; therefore glorify God in your body and in your spirit, which are God's"* (1 Corinthians 6:19–20, NKJV). In other words, I am a steward of my body. I was taught that as smoking could be harmful to my body (temple) I should avoid doing it. And I did! Imagine, spiritual leaders had reached that conclusion decades before the medical profession *finally* arrived at the same conclusion. I thank God that I never smoked once, even though my dad was a chain smoker.

### Key 2: Eat Nutritiously

I am not a trained nutritionist, but I have come to the conclusion that my body requires certain foods to be healthy. The T. H. Chan School of Public Health at Harvard lays it out perfectly in their Healthy Eating Plate guide. The main message: focus on diet quality. I quote,

> What's most important is the *type of carbohydrate* you choose to eat because some sources are healthier than others. The *amount of carbohydrate* in the diet…is less important than the *type of carbohydrate* in the diet. For example, healthy, whole grains such as whole wheat bread, rye, barley and quinoa are better choices than highly refined white bread or French fries.[8]

All of these foods put fibre into our systems, which is *absolutely essential* for good health.

We also need to limit red meat, processed meat and all foods that put too much sugar or salt into our bodies. A 2002 WHO (World Health Organization) report stated that people who eat meat should moderate their consumption of it, which is good advice for anything we eat. Health experts have stated that the amount of red meat we eat at a meal should not exceed the size of the palm of our hand. According to Eating Right Ontario, fish is recommended twice a week, as it is a low-fat high-quality protein, filled with omega-3 fatty acids and vitamins D and B12.[9]

To eat nutritiously we also needs lots of salads, but easy on the toppings as some of them are loaded with salt and sugar. Nuts of all kinds (saltless) are also very nutritious.

Eating nutritiously also involves limiting our intake of fruit juices and pop (usually loaded with sugar) and drinking lots of water. Nephrologist Stephen Guest, adjunct professor at Stanford University, says there are many benefits of practising a high intake of water.[10]

1. Bodily fluids affect our digestion, circulation, transportation of nutrients and maintenance of body temperature. Fluid losses are occurring throughout the day, and these losses need to be replaced for good health. Dehydration is a very serious matter.
2. Water helps energize muscles.
3. Water keeps skin healthy.
4. Water helps the kidneys function properly, cleansing and ridding our bodies of toxins, and may help us to avoid kidney stones.

Of course it needs to be said that there are hydration benefits received from any fluids that we drink, but the best one, and least expensive, is water—just cool, clear water!

---

[8] "Carbohydrates," Harvard T. H. Chan School of Public Health, accessed April 25, 2017, https://www.hsph.harvard.edu/nutritionsource/carbohydrates/.

[9] See www.eatrightontario.ca.

[10] Kathleen M. Zelman, "Six Reasons to Drink Water," WebMD, accessed April 25, 2017, http://www.webmd.com/diet/features/6-reasons-to-drink-water#1.

What also needs to be said about eating nutritiously is that there are occasional times in our life when we just need to throw good nutrition (including the facts on the label about sugar, saturated fats and calories) to the wind! As the biblical proverb says, *"There is a time for everything"* (Ecclesiastes 3:1), and this includes yielding once in a while to the temptation to just go ahead and enjoy, like enjoying one of those unhealthy hotdogs at a ball game, and of course smothered with unhealthy condiments. It also includes enjoying an occasional sumptuous buffet. Everything in life *in balance!*

### Key 3: Exercise Regularly

> Lack of activity destroys the good condition of every human being, while movement and methodical physical exercise save it and preserve it.[11]

Our bodies were created to be in motion. If you've ever had to spend a long period in bed, you will know how quickly our muscles can become flabby, weak and even atrophied. It is absolutely necessary then to be involved in some form of exercise or stretching *every day.* This does not have to be in a gym or an exercise class (though both are excellent ways to get exercise); we can just follow simple routines in our home. We can do stretches while we sit and watch television or put music on (*Time to Sing* videos on YouTube are excellent and inspiring) and just move to the beat, which is what I do every morning and often throughout the day. Also, while my oatmeal cereal is cooking for three minutes in the microwave, I do stretches. *Any exercise is better than none!* We should continue to participate in active games as much as possible, as they are fun and keep us moving. Walking for 20 to 30 minutes is good but should be considered only as the first step (pardon the pun) in an exercise program because it does not provide movement of every muscle in the body.

Our bodies have hundreds of muscle pairs. This means that the same muscle is on both the right and left side and also means that when we do stretches we must *always* do them on both sides of our body.

I highly recommend the book *End Back Pain Forever* by Norman Marcus.[12] It is a masterpiece on how to get rid of back pain and possibly avoid surgery and even *prevent* chronic pain in the first place. The theme of the book is muscle strengthening. The book offers 21 exercises for low back pain and also

---

[11] Plato, quoted in "Plato," Conservapedia, http://www.conservapedia.com/Plato.

[12] Norman Marcus, *End Back Pain Forever: A Groundbreaking Approach to Eliminate Your Suffering* (New York: Atria Books, 2012).

advocates very strongly doing deep breathing while exercising. My passionate interest in this subject of exercising regularly is explained in the following story.

## MY BACK PAIN STORY

In 1957 I was tobogganing with our youth group. The youth in my parish loved to have their pastor participating with them in activities. And of course I loved it too! I boarded a toboggan with one of my youth, and we were the first to try out the hill. Little did we know that partway down the hill there was a massive ice patch. When we hit it, we were spun down the hill at an uncontrollable speed. At the bottom on the hill we ran into a declivity and came to a shocking and literally back-breaking stop. I was thrown over 16-year-old Arthur, and we both ended up on our backs. Of course I screamed loudly for the other youth not to come down the hill. I was able to get up, but Arthur was in too much pain to even move. He was taken to the hospital and diagnosed with a broken back. He spent six weeks in hospital and months in rehab.

I had a few broken ribs and felt okay for a period of time. I still taught the youth Bible class on Sunday and led and preached at both worship services. However, as time went on I realized that I hadn't got off as easy as I thought. I began to have intense back pain. I went to a chiropractor and followed his instructions for many weeks. However, the pain did not subside; in fact it increased greatly. I decided I would just have to live with it as best I could, and I continued all my necessary day-to-day activities, my pastoral activities, and hoped that someday and somehow I would be able to get back to enjoying all the sporting activities I have always loved so much.

Four years later I commenced a new pastorate in Hamilton. I went to see a new family physician about my back pain and told him that I had suffered with it for four years and what had precipitated it. Immediately he recommended that I see an orthopaedic surgeon by the name of Dr. Hoffman, the doctor for the Hamilton Tiger-Cats football team, and an appointment was made.

Dr. Hoffman asked me for some background on my problem, and I told him about the tobogganing incident. Also he wanted to do know what steps I had taken to get relief. I told him everything my family physician in Barrie had tried and also what a chiropractor had tried, none of which had alleviated my pain. He sent me for X-rays.

On the next visit Dr. Hoffman informed me that I had developed scoliosis (a curvature in my spine), which was causing the pain. He then looked me in the eye and said, "Reverend, the first thing I need from you is a *commitment* that you will do exactly what I prescribe for you."

My response was immediate: "I certainly will, Doctor!"

He then described his plan. He said, "I want you to come to my office once a week for six months to receive short-wave treatments and then do my prescribed muscle-strengthening stretches twice a day. I can assure you that if you commit to that, you will be rid of your back pain in six to nine months; and if you continue these stretches for the rest of your life, you will never have major back pain again."

That sounded wonderful to me, as I was only in my early thirties and I didn't want to live out the rest of my life in such excruciating and life-affecting pain. As Dr. Hoffman knew I was a preacher and that my sermon preparations could involve sitting for long periods of time, he advised me to not ever sit for longer than 30 minutes and to get up and walk around. I have tried to follow his advice throughout my life, and I believe it has paid off.

After six months I experienced considerable relief, and at the end of nine months I was totally free of back pain. By continuing my daily muscle-strengthening stretches for the past 55 years I have never again had any major back pain, even though I played hockey into my late forties, skied into my eighties, and climbed ladders for 18 years in my decorating business. No wonder I am such a passionate advocate of daily exercises. Exercising regularly and keeping active benefit us in many ways:

1. Strengthens our muscles
2. Stimulates our minds
3. Speeds up our metabolism, which burns off calories

Regular exercising will also help control weight, combat type 2 diabetes, prevent falls, improve moods and promote better sleep, a subject I cover in key 5.

It's interesting that the exercises Dr. Hoffman prescribed for me are some of the very ones that Dr. Marcus prescribes in his book.

## POSTURE

This is a perfect place to talk about the importance of posture. Whether sitting or standing we should always be as erect as possible and avoid leg-crossing, as that can put our hips into a torqued position and can lead to back pain.

## Key 4: Brain-Stimulating Activities

Just as exercise helps our musculoskeletal system stay strong, so activities of many kinds help keep our brain healthy and strong. As senescence (deterioration due to aging) becomes more and more a reality in our lives, we need to do *everything in our power* to slow its progression. Regular exercise can stimulate the production of brain chemicals, such as serotonin and dopamine, which act as neurotransmitters in the brain and can improve our mental acuity. There are many activities beside physical exercise that we can get involved in to help make these chemical reactions happen, such as the following:

- Word games (Jumble Words, Scrabble, Sudoku, Find the Word)
- Brain twisters
- Puzzles
- Learning new computer skills (I never stop learning them)
- A variety of reading (I always have three or four books on various subjects on the-go)
- Research on anything and everything
- Card games, colouring (not just for children anymore!)
- Woodworking (a lifetime passion for me)
- Gardening (Carolyn's mom did it into her nineties)
- Dancing (as the song says, "Dance, dance, wherever you are")
- Socializing (we need to be with people, even it's just for coffee or tea)
- Sports activities of all kinds

A report out of the University of British Columbia Okanagan's School of Health and Exercise Sciences, written by Professor Kathleen Martin Ginis, says,

> "After evaluating all the research available, our panel agrees that physical activity is a practical, economical and accessible intervention for both the prevention and management of Alzheimer's disease and other dementias."… The team concluded that older adults not diagnosed with Alzheimer's who are physically active were significantly less likely to develop the disease compared to those who were inactive.[13]

My advice to everyone over 40 is to *just keep moving physically and mentally!* Our bodies and minds were designed for *movement.*

## Key 5: Get A Good Night's Sleep

> True silence is the rest of the mind and is to the spirit what sleep is to the body, nourishment and refreshment.[14]

---

[13] Paulina Wu, "Exercise associated with reduced risk of Alzheimer's disease: Study," Global News, May 16, 2017, http://globalnews.ca/news/3455321/exercise-associated-with-reduced-risk-of-alzheimers-disease-study/.

[14] William Penn, "William Penn's Advice to His Children," QHPress, http://www.qhpress.org/quakerpages/qwhp/advice2.htm.

The Bible indicates that God is concerned about us working too hard and not getting a good sleep. The Psalmist says, "It is foolish for you to work so hard from early morning to late at night, anxiously working for food to eat, when God is waiting to give you—His beloved—a good night's sleep" (Psalm 127:2, my paraphrase).

### ARE THE RIGHT MATTRESS AND PILLOW THE SOLUTION TO SLEEPLESSNESS?

The ads try to convince us that all we need to get a good night's sleep are the right mattress and pillow. But they will not give us a good rest if we lie down with a restless spirit.

In an article in the *Toronto Star*, feature writer Francine Kopun tells us that the most expensive mattress in Toronto costs $93,000. It's a king-size mattress made from horsehair harvested from black stallions in Argentina. "Each mattress is precisely crafted to fit the size, shape and sleeping habits of each buyer."[15] I wonder, is that plus tax of over $12,000? Do the buyers actually get a better night's sleep? What happens when the size and shape of the buyers change?

I love that expression "sleep like a baby." I can remember so well looking at the faces of my sons when they were asleep and thinking that it was the most beautiful sight one could ever behold. Little children fall off to sleep when they feel sure that Mommy or Daddy is nearby and watching over them. We too, as children of God, have a Heavenly Father watching over us and caring for us, whether we are awake or asleep. The Psalmist writes, *"My help comes from the LORD, the Maker of heaven and earth. He will not let your foot slip—he who watches over you will not slumber; indeed, he who watches over Israel will neither slumber nor sleep"* (Psalm 121:2–4). *"In peace I will lie down and sleep, for you alone, LORD, make me dwell in safety"* (Psalm 4:8).

### TRYING TO SOLVE THE PROBLEM OF SLEEPLESSNESS

Problems getting to sleep are experienced by a large percentage of the population of every age group. Consequently many go to their physician, who will in many cases try to solve the problem through medication. This works for a little while but can also result in serious side effects. Pharmacists in Canada can fill up to 5.6 million prescriptions for sleeping pills in a year.[16]

---

[15] Francine Kopun, "A mattress for every taste," *Toronto Star*, March 10, 2011, https://www.thestar.com/life/homes/decor/2011/03/10/a_mattress_for_every_taste.html.

[16] "Is Canada addicted to sleeping pills?," *Best Health Magazine*, April 2011, accessed April 25, 2017, http://www.besthealthmag.ca/best-you/sleep/is-canada-addicted-to-sleeping-piss/ .

Others attend one of the ever proliferating sleep disorder clinics. These too may help some, but perhaps there is a simpler method that could be put into practice in order to get a good night's rest and sleep. I am going to share with you my method, which has worked for me for many years and even when going through traumatic experiences.

## MY PREPARATION FOR A GOOD NIGHT'S REST AND SLEEP

It's interesting that we are in the habit of preparing for many things in life and yet do not give any thought to how we can prepare for a good night's sleep. Here are seven things I do to prepare:

1. Have my big meal at noon.
2. Limit my daytime snooze to 20–30 minutes.
3. No caffeine after 3 p.m.
4. No watching late-night news of the world.
5. No television in my bedroom.
6. No reading in bed and of course no using an iPhone (if I had one).
7. Follow as much as possible a going-to-bed routine.

As specialists advocate that children should have a bedtime routine, so all of us should follow going-to bed and getting-up routines. Our bodies have a *biological clock*—called the circadian rhythm—and it is at our *sleep peril* to not follow it. The circadian rhythm tells us when to sleep and when to wake up.

My wife Carolyn's dad—who got up at 4:30 a.m. every day for 40 years to milk the cows—had an answer to how much sleep we need to put in an honest day's work the next day: "If you need an alarm clock to wake you up, you're going to bed too late."

## MY IN-BED ROUTINE

The first thing I do when I hop into bed is to thank God for all His blessings bestowed so freely upon me that day. The Psalmist wrote, "*I will extol the LORD at all times; his praise will always be on my lips*" (Psalm 34:1). That puts me in a positive and relaxed mood and precludes my mind getting into any burdensome things that may have happened during the day. I then thank God for His promise to give me a good night's rest and sleep (Psalm 127:2). My third step is to get into my "hymn routine"—a litany of hymns I have known for decades that express trust in God, like "Be Still My Soul," "Tis So Sweet to Trust in Jesus," "Simply Trusting Every Day," "It Is Well with My Soul" and "Like a River Glorious."The words of the latter one—written by Frances R. Havergal—are so very fitting for helping me to get into a restful sleep every night.

Like a river glorious is God's perfect peace
Over all victorious, in its bright increase
Perfect, yet it floweth fuller every day,
Perfect, yet it groweth deeper all the way.

Stayed upon Jehovah, hearts are fully blest
Finding, as He promised, perfect peace and rest.

By filling my mind with *positive* spiritual truths like these, I leave no room for anxious thoughts about what may be ahead the next day. I am *transcending* my thoughts above anything that could cause my mind to get into a restless state. Soon I am drifting off into a beautiful night's rest and sleep, just as my Heavenly Father promised (Psalm 127:2).

### Key 6: A Positive Outlook on Life

"The pessimist says the day will be partly cloudy; the optimist says the day will be partly sunny" (a Nully Nugget). The emphasis is on our outlook, which means that if we are going to see the glass as half full (or, better still, as full) we will need to learn to do the following:

1. Stop looking at those who seem to be better off than we are, and start looking around at those who are so much worse off than we are (think of refugee camps).
2. Look around and see and revel in all the little blessings we *have*, rather than dwelling on the ones we *don't have*.
3. Be a blessing to someone each day in some little way, bringing a smile to their face or, even better, a laugh. "The purpose of life is to be a blessing to others; that will bring happiness to ourselves and to others" (a Nully Nugget).

Often when out and about I will say something uplifting and positive to people I meet, such as "What a glorious sunny day." I am always saddened when the response is something like: "Yes, it is, *but* it won't last." These are "buts" that we need to delete from our vocabulary and our spirit as they do not contribute to us developing a positive outlook on life. I often feel like saying (but my pastoral wisdom tells me not to), "Let's just enjoy *this* beautiful day to the full!"

Too many people live their *present* through the hurts of the *past*. I hope that you have concluded by now that this book you hold in your hands is *not* an invitation to a "pity party." Yes, I have—like everyone else—experienced many hurts in the past. However, wallowing in those hurts is not going to result in me living the abundant life that Jesus promised His followers would have (John 10:10). "*Forgetting what is behind*"—the apostle Paul wrote—"*and straining toward what is ahead*" (Philippians 3:13). *That* should be the goal of our lives!

## Key 7: Making Time for Reflection and Meditation

Notice that I have used the verb "making," as the decision to set apart time to be still and quiet requires effort and determination. That is why the Psalmist makes it clear that it is the Shepherd who leads him to the place of "*quiet waters*" (Psalm 23:2). Sometimes in our hectic lives, we need a friend to insist that we cut back on our activities or we need a circumstance that forces us to do so. The latter was my experience.

### NO TIME FOR REFLECTION AND MEDITATION

In my late twenties I was one going concern. The story of how I led my congregation into relocating and a new building program is in part 1, chapter 1. Anyone who has been through that will know that it is a very time- and energy-demanding experience. All that time I was still involved in my many pastoral responsibilities: preparation of sermons; preaching at two Sunday services (with the evening service being broadcast on radio); teaching the Sunday morning youth Bible class; teaching at the mid-week Bible study and prayer meeting; preparing and conducting my weekly "Good News" radio broadcast; visiting the sick in homes, hospitals and nursing homes; officiating at weddings and marriages; and itinerant preaching. The latter included engagements lined up to be the guest preacher at a week of youth outreach services in a church in Simcoe, Ontario, and camp pastor for two weeks at a Christian youth camp in Muskoka. On top of all my pastoral duties were my responsibilities as a husband and father.

The result of trying to keep up with all this activity was burnout, a condition that will be familiar to many professionals and businesspeople. Yes, as the saying goes, "One *can* burn the candle at both ends, but the result will always be a meltdown." My system had a major meltdown. A virus entered my bloodstream that put me in hospital for two weeks, followed by two months of bedrest at home. For two months following that I was only able to meet my pastoral duties part-time. As the saying goes, my get-up-and-go had got-up-and-gone.

I was blessed during this time of hospitalization and recuperation to have an excellent, highly qualified youth pastor—Paul Fawcet—who took over my duties and did an amazing job. It was my desire of course to get back to my pastoral and preaching duties as soon as possible, but as I was under the care of our excellent family physician, Dr. John Postnikoff, it was to be his decision and not mine.

## A LESSON LEARNED

It was all a great lesson for me, one that would help me the rest of my life to remember that these bodies and minds of ours have limits, however young or healthy we may be. My family physician helped me to understand what I needed to do to avoid getting burned out again. At a meeting in his office, he turned to me and said, "Reverend, if you don't start taking time off for yourself and your family, you may not reach your thirtieth birthday." That was a wake-up call! He then took his prescription pad in hand and said, "I am going to write out a prescription for you—not for more *medication* but for more *meditation*." He was actually speaking from his own personal experience as one of the busiest physicians in Simcoe County who had himself experienced burnout. He continued, "I want you to inform your board of elders and church members that your doctor has prescribed that you take a day off, completely free of your pastoral duties, and that you set time aside for your own reflection and meditation every day." I followed his prescription—took a day off each week to do fun things with my family and returned to having a daily quiet time, as I had been taught as a youth by the spiritual leaders of our church. I have continued to this day, over 60 years later. Quiet time—as many Christians referred to it years ago—is a time set aside every day to read a passage of Scripture, meditate on it, and then spend time in prayer and praise.

## THE BIBLE AND QUIET TIMES

The Bible has some powerful and practical things to say about the *need* we have for quiet times in our busy lives:

1. "*Be still, and know that I am God*" (Psalm 46:10). It seems that even after declaring that "*God is our refuge and strength, A very present help in trouble*" (vs. 1, NKJV) and that "*the God of Jacob is our fortress*" (vs. 7) the Psalmist's mind must still be in turmoil over what is happening among the nations of the world. He desperately needs to hear from God, and he does. The still small voice of the Lord comes to him (as it comes to us often): "Be still, and remember who I am! Trust me—I am the Sovereign One—I can take care of what is happening in the world." It reminds me of a saying I read, "For peace of mind, we need to resign as general manager of the universe." How true! When our son Eric was a little fellow, we were sitting around the table after a meal (as has always been a custom of our family), having a discussion about this and that. All of a sudden he turned to his mom and said, "Mommy, I think Daddy would like to run the whole world." Little minds! Great insight!
   Each night as I pillow my head, I ask God to say to my spirit, "Be still, and know that I am God." Soon my spirit is at rest, and I am off to sleep.
2. "*Yes, my soul, find rest in God*" (Psalm 62:5). When we learn to wait upon God in our quiet times, He will impart to our spirits the rest that only He can give and the kind of rest our minds, bodies and spirits need.

3. *"Come with me by yourselves to a quiet place and get some rest"* (Mark 6:31). The reason why Jesus instructed His disciples to retreat to a quiet place for rest is explained in the text: *"So many people were coming and going that they did not even have a chance to eat."* All of us over-achieving people can relate to that. We may grab a bite or a coffee at a fast food outlet to gulp down, but it isn't going to do us much good; in fact, such a practice may lead to our system coming apart at the seams.

## COME APART OR COME APART

When I returned to the pulpit following my illness, I entitled the first sermon I preached "Come apart or you *will* come apart." We all know the experience of owning a garment that through much wear and tear and laundering begins to fall apart at the seams. That is a perfect metaphor for what happens in our lives when we rush around and fail to observe quiet times, as you have read about happening in my life.

## A RUSHING SOCIETY

Who would ever deny that we live in a society in which people are moving at a pace that past generations knew nothing about? We drive vehicles at speeds many times what our forefathers drove, and we often exceed the designated speed limit, hoping not to be pulled over by a police officer.

When we are driving on the highway, we have to wonder what the drivers who are swerving in and out are going to do with all that time they are saving. The jury is still out as to whether speed is the number-one factor in vehicle accidents. However, whether it is or not, it is probably true that when we are driving at faster speeds, our mind is also racing more as we are driving distracted, worrying about getting to our destination late or being pulled over. It is indeed better to arrive *late* than to arrive *dead*.

For many people their day could be encapsulated in the words "rushing around." They rush out of bed, rush through their shower, rush into their outfit for the day, rush through their breakfast (or rush to their car and pick up a coffee on the way to work). They rush into work and rush around all day at work, rush back into their car and rush home. They rush to get dinner ready (or rush to put on the table the food they have picked up at a fast food outlet), rush to get ready to go out to an evening activity, after they have rushed the kids into bed in preparation for the sitter, who comes rushing in at the last second. They rush home and rush to bed! They then wonder why they can't get to sleep. (See key 5, Get a Good Night's Sleep.)

## CHILDREN AND RUSHING AROUND

Children today are living at a pace unknown to those of us of a past generation.

We see parents picking up their children after school, rushing them into the car and rushing them off to yet another after-school activity. How I thank God that I was brought up in a generation in which my parents allowed me to come home from school and just create my own fun, with absolutely no rushing around to appointments for this and that. Parents today need to learn to *let kids be kids* and create their *own* leisure time fun and activities. As I often walk by the nearby elementary school on my way to the coffee shop when the students are outside for recess, I take note of the many ways the children are entertaining themselves, just thinking up games as they go along. That is what my childhood was like, and that is what the childhood of every child should be like!

## THE TOLL OF RUSHING AROUND

It is natural and normal to experience a certain level of stress throughout our daily activities, and at such a level, the stress we experience is not only harmless but necessary to the carrying out of our daily tasks.

However, when our stress levels reach the chronic stage, they are *not harmless* to our health and well-being. Many studies have shown that chronic stress may lead to health problems, such as anxiety, depression, viral illnesses, common colds, alcohol or drug abuse, overeating or undereating, and more.

Dr. Hans Selye was known as the father of stress research. He was born in Vienna, Austria, and came to Canada to do research at McGill University in Montreal. He became a distinguished endocrinologist, writing some 1,700 articles and 43 books on the subject of stress. His most widely read book was *Stress Without Distress*, in which he advanced the theory that stress plays a role in every disease, including ulcers, high blood pressure and heart attacks.[17]

Our Lord Jesus is our perfect example of needing to get away from the pressures of life. In the Gospel according to Mark we read, "*Because so many people kept coming and going that they did not even have a chance to eat, he said to them, 'Come with me by yourselves to a quiet place and get some rest*" (Mark 6:31). Notice that Jesus didn't instruct His disciples to go on their *own* to get rest; He invited them to come along with Him. We all need times of rest away from the demands of life. That has become much more difficult in our society with our cellphones turned on constantly, but we have the choice to turn them off occasionally just so that we are not always "on call."

---

[17] Hans Selye, *Stress Without Distress* (n.p.: McClelland and Stewart, 1974).

When God instructed His people to *"Remember the Sabbath Day by keeping it holy"* (Exodus 20:8), it was *not* the *period of time* that was most important but the *principle* that everyone needs a period of time away from their usual work. God (as did Jesus) set an example when *"in six days the* LORD *made the heavens and the earth, the sea, and all that is in them, but* **he rested** *on the seventh day"* (Exodus 20:11, emphasis added). We can make light of the "Sabbath Day Principle" and flaunt it if we so choose, but we will pay the cost for doing so! These human bodies were not meant to keep going seven days and nights a week!

WAYS TO PREVENT GETTING STRESSED OUT

The old saying "An ounce of prevention is worth a pound of cure" is applicable here. Unfortunately it's human nature to not even think about prevention until we are forced to (as in my case in my late twenties).

The Internet lists a whole plethora of recommended programs for relieving stress. The problem with most of these is that they are too complicated and drawn out for the average person to even think of following. They range from "10 Ways" to "79 Ways" to relieve stress. As in so many areas of life, we need to follow the KISS principle: "Keep It Super Simple." Here is how I keep my stress-relieving program super simple:

1. Keeping my daily spiritual quiet time, as described previously.
2. Breathing deeply. I sit erect with both feet on the floor, close my eyes, inhale through my nose to the count of eight, and then exhale through my mouth. I repeat this at least ten times. This is a great and simple stress reliever for those sitting at a desk or computer all day and for all business executives and professionals.
3. Listening to quiet, light music and losing myself in the rhythm.
4. Visualizing, in which I imagine I am sitting on a beach watching the sunrise or sunset or any experience that brings pleasure to my mind.
5. Progressive relaxing, which is more active but a great stress reliever. Start with tensing and relaxing foot muscles, and work all muscles on the way up to your neck and head. Time-consuming to be sure, but in time you will feel the amazing beneficial effects of it. Muscles are meant to be moved, and when they are not they will become deactivated and dormant, and we will suffer the consequences. Or as the old maxim puts it, "Use them or lose them."
6. Walking, preferably outdoors to gain the benefit of fresh air and to enjoy the surroundings.
7. Keeping lightened up—see pillar 2, A Light Spirit—and always remembering that life is too short to take it too seriously (a Nully Nugget)!

## A Word About Massage and Physiotherapy

As I have been a very active person since my childhood and have at times been unwise about the way I have treated my body (skiing too fast and out of control for example) it has been necessary for me to receive help from professional therapists. They have been an incredible help in getting me back to normal and free of the pain I was feeling.

However, it is important to say this about therapists: They cannot do it all for us; we must be willing to do *our* part, and that is where the rub comes in. Any therapist worth going to will assign certain stretches for their patient to do between appointments and will follow up to make sure the patient is *doing* the prescribed stretches. A therapist once told me that I was her only patient who was carrying through the stretching assignments from her. It is no wonder that so many seniors experience so many muscle pains throughout their bodies. Muscles need to be worked, and it *is* work to keep them supple, but well worth it!

## A Word About Keeping Muscles Warm

Some years ago, following an injury from a skiing accident, I went to a physiotherapist for a series of adjustments, and she gave me a piece of advice that I have never forgotten and have practised daily for all these years. She said, "Ernie, you can never put too much heat on a sore muscle." I purchased a Magic Bag, which I heat in the microwave and use every time I am in a sitting position for a period of time. It has worked wonders! I have been through several bags and would never be without one. I urge all seniors, in particular, to keep those sore muscles warm!

## A Word About Use of Cellphones

As one looks around in public at people on their cellphones one has to conclude that society is going to require an exponential proliferation of therapists to care for those who spent years on their phones in a slouching position. Our bodies were meant to be in the erect position when sitting, and that is a far cry from most cellphone users I see in public. Poor posture has a way of catching up with us, sooner or later. Added to this problem will be the arthritis that will potentially take its toll on the fingers and wrists of cellphone users. I know something about excruciating pain from arthritis in one's hands, mine caused by 18 years of wallpapering in my decorating business.

## A Final Word on Slowing Down

Have you ever noticed—as I have—that so often when we pass a vehicle, lo and behold there it is right beside us at the next red light? One wonders what we think we can gain by gaining all those seconds. We seem to be a society *driven*— pardon the pun—by the false assumption that, because life seems to be moving by us so quickly, we need always to speed up. Let each of us determine to take time to smell the roses and just sip our cup of tea or coffee. Simon and Garfunkel captured this thought perfectly when they wrote "The 59th Street Bridge Song (Feelin' Groovy)" with the words "Slow down, you move too fast."

## PILLAR 6: AN ALTRUISTIC SPIRIT

Benjamin Franklin wrote, "People who are wrapped up in themselves make small packages."[18] What a different society we would live in if we all put into action the principle that our Lord articulated in the story of the good Samaritan (Luke 10:25–37). The religious scholar wanted to know from Jesus how he could inherit eternal life. The answer Jesus gave is far different than the one most of us evangelical preachers would have given! We (myself included) would have gotten into a homily about being born again, but Jesus' answer was all about *reaching out to our neighbour*. Jesus then clarified *who* our neighbour is: It's that man travelling from Jerusalem to Jericho who was robbed, stripped of his clothes, beaten and left to die. So if we apply that situation to ourselves, it's the person we come across in our busy daily lives who has a need to be met, a need that is beyond *their* means and ability to meet but within *our* ability and means to meet. The story is told of a priest who was sent by his bishop to work in the slums of a city. When the priest arrived, he looked around and gasped, "Lord, what are You going to do about this appalling situation?" The Lord replied, "That's what I sent you here for."

The priest in Jesus' story *saw* the man and passed by on the other side; the Levite (an assistant to a priest) *saw* the man and passed by; but the Samaritan (not a mainstream Jew) *saw* the man and behaved differently! What made the difference? *He* saw the man through the lens of his heart as a person in need whose need he was able and willing to take time out from his busy schedule to meet. He showed mercy, which means "kindness or help given to people who are in a very bad or desperate situation" (*Merriam Webster Learner's Dictionary*). Isn't that what God's love is all about, reaching out and down to "save a wretch like me" as John Newton put it in "Amazing Grace"?

The questions we need to answer are, what would *I* have done? Would *I* be so wrapped up in my own plans and the needs of my own family and friends that I would ignore the needs of the man: beaten, bruised and bloody? Would I have given this stranger the TLC the Samaritan gave him? These are serious questions, because Jesus taught in the parable that if I don't do these things I will *not* inherit eternal life!

If we find that difficult to accept, we need to pay heed to what Jesus taught as recorded in Matthew 25:31–46, in the story of the sheep and goats. Jesus made

---

[18] Benjamin Franklin, *Poor Richard's Almanack*.

it clear that the sheep are those who reach out to the needy and meet their needs. The goats in Jesus' story were those who did not do these things! The needy in the story are those who are hungry, thirsty, homeless, in need of clothes, sick or in prison. The *strength* of evangelicals is the emphasis we put on the factor of grace in salvation (Ephesians 2:8–9); the *weakness* is the lack of emphasis we put on the *outworking* of that grace (Ephesians 2:10). We are saved not just to *share the gospel* but also to *share our goods* with those who have so much less!

When we arrive at the Pearly Gates, Jesus is not going to ask us how often we attended church or what we believed about eschatology, Calvinism, Israel or the inspiration of Scriptures. He will ask us how many cups of cold water we gave out and how many hungry people we help feed.

So what should all this mean to me as I go about just trying to live out my life each day? It should mean that *every day* I will seek God's guidance as to whom I should reach out to and be a blessing to. I need to remember this Nully Nugget: "The purpose of life is to be a blessing to others."

As one of the founders of the Barrie and District Christmas Cheer, little did I know the measure of joy that I would experience as a result of giving my time, energy and leadership skills—without reserve and remuneration—to bring joy into the lives of thousands of families not so blessed as mine. This organization collects, assembles and distributes food and toy hampers to less-fortunate families of Simcoe County and does it all through hundreds of volunteers. It was my honour and privilege to be the president of this organization for 28 years. Skeptics (we'll always have those with us when it comes to reaching out to the less fortunate) would ask, "Do these people *appreciate* what you do for them?" I would respond, "If you could read the letters of thanks I receive you would have the answer to your question. Letters like 'Dear Rev. Nullmeyer: Our family wouldn't have had a Christmas if it weren't for you and your wonderful volunteers. My children could not have been happier with the toys your volunteers chose for them.'" Wow! That made it all worthwhile! Other skeptics wondered if these people were *worthy* of our efforts. My response was "I guess some people thought that when our family of ten children received the Toronto Star Christmas boxes back in the Depression" and "Are any of us worthy of the blessings that we have received although we did nothing to deserve them?" Mother Teresa had a powerful response to skeptics: "If you judge people, you will have no time to love them."[19] She also gave us this wonderful thought: "If you can't feed a hundred people then just feed one."[20] If there was ever a person

---

[19] Mother Teresa, quoted in *Quotations for all Occasions* (Emerald Publishers, 2009).

[20] Mother Teresa, quoted in David Ruis, *The Justice God Is Seeking* (Grand Rapids: Bethany House, 2006).

who lived like Jesus to bless the less fortunate, it was Mother Teresa! She would have loved the well-known starfish story, which is worth repeating here.

A young man is walking along the ocean and sees a beach on which thousands of starfish have washed ashore. Farther along, he sees an old man walking slowly and stooping often, picking up one starfish after another and tossing each one gently into the ocean. "Why are you throwing starfish into the ocean?" he asks.

"Because the sun is up and the tide is going out and if I don't throw them farther in they will die."

"But, old man, don't you realize there are miles and miles of beach and starfish all along it? You can't possibly save them all. You can't even save one-tenth of them. In fact, if you worked all day, your efforts wouldn't make any difference at all!"

The old man listens calmly and then bends down to pick up another starfish and throw it into the sea as he says, *"It made a difference to that one!"*

## Making a Difference

Ah yes, the difference we could make in our society if each and every one of us did everything we could to be a blessing to those not as blessed as we are! Each evening when readying for bed I ask myself, what did I do today to help lift someone's burden? That is, to bring blessing into someone's life because of the way God has so abundantly blessed me beyond anything I deserve! Did I bless people with a smile, a funny story to give them a laugh, a compliment, a word of encouragement, a gift of money, an expression of gratitude, a word of comfort, a phone call, a note or e-mail? And the list could go on. It is true that people will forget what I said (which is rather humbling after preaching over 5,000 sermons), but they will never forget that *one little act of kindness* I did for them and how I made them feel.

God said to Abraham, "I will bless you *so that* you may be a blessing" (Genesis 12:2, my paraphrase and emphasis). That's why God blesses some of us so much, so that we can *pass on* some of that blessing to others who are not so blessed! Jesus said to His disciples and thus to us, *"Freely you have received; freely give"* (Matthew 10:8). How tempting it is for those us who have been freely blessed with this world's goods to use them all for ourselves or for our families and friends. God wants us to pass on some of that blessing to others who are not so blessed!

## What Would Jesus Do?

Every day of the week a blind man set up his fruit cart on the main street of a town in order to earn a few extra dollars. One day he heard what sounded like a group of youth coming near and just laughing and having a fun time together. He didn't know what they were laughing about, but he was soon to find out. They had on their minds what they thought would be a fun thing to do.

Presently he heard the youth scream out, "Okay, let's do it!" With one accord they pushed over his fruit stand, sending the fruit rolling all over the street. He then heard them running away, laughing. He thought to himself, *Maybe some kind person will come by and help me pick up my fruit cart and put the fruit back in place.* To his deep disappointment, he could hear footsteps of people hurrying by—maybe on their cellphones—but no one taking the time to stop and help him.

However, presently he was aware of someone stopping and asking, "What happened?" Before he could get the answer out, the person was busy righting his fruit cart and putting the fruit back in place. After the "Good Samaritan" said, "There, everything's back in place now," the fruit vendor blurted out, "You must be Jesus!"

Well, to be sure it wasn't Jesus in the *flesh*, but it was Jesus in the *spirit*. Often, during our Lord's earthly sojourn, He stopped—while on the way somewhere— to reach out and be a blessing to someone He met along the way who was in need of a blessing.

The question is, would you have been that person who did what Jesus would have done? Would I have been? May God give each and every one of us the "spirit of Jesus" to be willing to stop on our way somewhere to bestow a blessing on someone in need.

I have heard many people say when the conversation turns to helping the poor, "Charity begins at home."

"Yes," I respond, "but it should not *end* there." And the reason is that there is a plethora of passages in the Bible about helping the needy. In fact there are more passages on this subject than on heaven and hell combined. And how often do we hear television preachers emphasizing the biblical truths on the subject of eschatology (end times) and saying so little about reaching out to the less fortunate of our society? Jesus summed in all up when He said to His disciples, "*Freely you have received; freely give*" (Matthew 10:8). Following are just a few of the many biblical passages about us reaching out to meet the needs of the needy.

"*There will always be poor people in the land. Therefore I command you to be openhanded toward your fellow Israelites who are poor and needy in your land*" (Deuteronomy 15:11). I have heard people interpret the first part of this passage of the Bible as saying "Well, so what? There are always going to be poor people in the world, and that is just the way it is." The following verse is an answer to that heartless comment: *"If anyone has material possessions and sees a brother or sister in need but has no pity on them, how can the love of God be in that person?"* (1 John 3:17).

*"Whoever is kind to the poor lends to the* LORD, *and he will reward them for what they have done"* (Proverbs 19:17).

> *Then Jesus said to his host, "When you give a luncheon or dinner, do not invite your friends, your brothers or sisters, your relatives, or your rich neighbors; if you do, they may invite you back and so you will be repaid. But when you give a banquet, invite the poor, the crippled, the lame, the blind, and you will be blessed. Although they cannot repay you, you will be repaid at the resurrection of the righteous."* (Luke 14:12–14)

We must always be sure that our giving to the less fortunate is done in a spirit of altruism, as our Lord illustrates it in the story of whom we invite to the feast we are providing. I must ask myself, Am I doing this good deed to look good in the eyes of the public? Or just to make myself feel warm and fuzzy? Or even just to get a tax refund? I had a parishioner who, when he received a refund, calculated how much of the return was a result of his charitable giving and then asked the Lord whom he should share it with. I had just commenced my first pastorate and didn't have many suits in my closet (in fact, just one!), so he had coffee with me one day and informed me that he was going to take me to a certain men's clothing store in downtown Hamilton (the best one in Hamilton, where he had his suits tailor-made) and have them fit me up for a new suit along with a new shirt and tie. Wow! Was I ever glad to wear that new outfit in the pulpit and when I officiated at weddings and funerals…and to have congregants tell me how nice I looked in it! Of course I did not reveal the source of the money that made it possible. That was a beautiful act of altruistic benevolence, and I have never forgotten this man's practical generosity to me.

*"Anyone who has been stealing must steal no longer, but must work, doing something useful with their own hands, that they may have something to share with those in need"* (Ephesians 4:28). Paul is admonishing those who have been living on stolen goods not just to get working instead of stealing but to work hard enough so that they will have enough money left over from their own *needs* to share with others.

*"If you spend yourselves on behalf of the hungry and satisfy the needs of the oppressed, then your light will rise in the darkness, and night will become like the noonday"* (Isaiah 58:10).

*"Do not forget to do good and to share with others, for with such sacrifices God is pleased"* (Hebrews 13:16).

*"If anyone gives even a cup of cold water to one of these little ones who is my disciple, truly I tell you, that person will certainly not lose their reward"* (Matthew 10:42).

As those who have blessed so *abundantly* with this world's goods, let us take *every* opportunity we can to bless those who have so much less.

"I cannot light up the whole world, but I can light up my little corner of that world" (a Nully Nugget). One of the songs we sang often in Sunday school when I was a boy was "Jesus Bids Us Shine."

> Jesus bids us shine with a clear, pure light
> Like a little candle burning in the night.
> In this world of darkness, we must shine
> You in your small corner, and I in mine.
> Susan B. Warner

## PILLAR 7: FAMILY AND FRIENDS
### Support of Family

How wonderful to be the patriarch of a closely knit family that loves one another, cares for one another, and gathers around one another in a special way when a traumatic situation arises. The Nullmeyer Clan (as I like to refer to us) is a family that enjoys hugging one another and can allow tears to flow when we experience sorrow as a family. I thank God for the way my family has reached out to me, particularly in recent times, with the passing of our dear family member and my beloved son Kevin and with Alzheimer's so deeply affecting our beloved Carolyn's life.

However, our family is also one that likes having lots of fun. At all our family gatherings much hilarity takes place. We all believe and practice my Nully Nugget that says "A light spirit will see us through the dark and heavy times of life." We are essentially a *very* lighthearted group of individuals. Thank God for that!

### Why God Established the Family

God established the family as *the* foundation of a society. How sad that this foundation has become so broken in so many families in our society.

There are over 50 *"one anothers"* in the New Testament, and all of them can be applied to family life. I shall list a few of them.

- *"Be devoted to one another in love"* (Romans 12:10).
- *"Live in harmony with one another"* (Romans 12:16).
- *"Be like-minded, be sympathetic, love one another"* (1 Peter 3:8).
- *"Accept one another, then, just as Christ accepted you"* (Romans 15:7).
- *"Serve one another humbly in love"* (Galatians 5:13).
- *"Do not lie to one another"* (Colossians 3:9, NKJV).
- *"Encouraging one another"* (Hebrews 10:25).
- *"Pray for one another"* (James 5:16, NKJV).
- *"Be kind and compassionate to one another"* (Ephesians 4:32).
- *"Bear one another's burdens"* (Galatians 6:2, NKJV).
- *"Greet one another with a holy kiss"* (Romans 16:16). There is much discussion among theologians as what this admonition actually means. The admonition is also made to the believers at Corinth (1 Corinthians 16:20; 2 Corinthians 13:12) and at Thessalonica (1 Thessalonians 5:26). I believe it means that when we come together as followers of Jesus we should express our love and care for another by some form of affection. I prefer to give a good warm hug with a verbal expression like "Lovely to see you again" or whatever comes to my mind at the time. I just want the person to know that it's a pleasure for me to see them again and that at that precise moment they are *very special* to me. It must also be remembered that some people are averse to being hugged (a few of my siblings were like that), and that feeling must be honoured. In those cases I give them a two-handed handshake, look them in the eye, and say something like I have suggested.
- *"Forgiving one another"* (Ephesians 4:32, NKJV). This is perhaps the most difficult "one another" in the Bible. When we consider the admonition to forgive one another—*within the context*—we would think that it would be natural and a simple matter to forgive others for those times when they have hurt our feelings with a word or action. We are to forgive one another *"just as in Christ God forgave you."* However, must of us know—*from experience*—that it isn't quite that simple! It seems to be human nature to enjoy holding grudges, especially if we believe we are in the right (which is of course most of the time!) and therefore the other person doesn't *deserve* our forgiveness. So then *we* are faced with the question, do *we* deserve to be forgiven for all the sins *we* have committed against God? Of course we don't! Then why should we feel that people do not deserve *our* forgiveness? I have known people—even people of faith—who have held grudges into their nineties for something someone said or did to them when they were children. Sad, oh so sad! They are *not* hurting the other person; they are *just hurting themselves.* The other and even more important aspect of forgiving one another is that if we *do not* forgive others for their sins against us, God will not—*will not,* that is—forgive us for the sins we commit against Him. That is serious stuff that is based upon God's Word and the words of our Lord Jesus in Matthew 6:12.

## Support of Friends

I feel so blessed to have so many friends—some of them dating back over 60 years—who have held me up in prayer and given me a word of encouragement when they have known I was going through tough times. The old adage is true: "A friend in need is a friend indeed." I also feel blessed when I can hold my friends up in prayer and speak a word of encouragement to them when they are going through challenging times. "I have learned that the best way to bear one's own burdens is to reach out and help someone else bear their burden" (a Nully Nugget).

## Thoughts About Friendship

- "A true friend walks in when others walk out."[21]
- "A true friend never gets in your way, unless you are going down."[22]
- "It's not a lack of love but a lack of friendship that makes unhappy marriages."[23]
- "Friends are those rare people who ask how we are and then wait to hear the answer."[24]
- "Lots of people want to ride with you in the limo, but a true friend will take the bus with you when the limo breaks down."[25]
- "A true friend is there for you in sunny times and also in stormy times" (a Nully Nugget).

Each and every day I thank God for the support of my beloved family and my dear friends.

---

[21] Walter Wrenwell, quoted in Tony Nolan, *Faith Fuel* (n.p.: Xulon Press, 2007), 103.

[22] H. Glasgow, quoted in Terry Nolan, *Faith Fuel*, 103.

[23] Friedrich Nietzsche, quoted in *Drum: A Magazine of Africa for Africa, Issues 754–762* (2007), 40.

[24] Ed Cunningham, quoted in Karen Casey, *The Good Stuff* (San Francisco: Conari Press, 2013), 115.

[25] Oprah Winfrey, source unknown.

# BAD THINGS AND GOD'S WILL

## THE SOVEREIGNTY OF GOD

Let me first declare that I believe that God is sovereign! The questions that emanate from that declaration include the following: Does God control every aspect of our lives? And thence does He cause bad things to happen in our lives? What does it really mean that God is sovereign? Do other factors such as acts of nature and randomness enter into the equation when bad things come storming into our lives? If we assert that God is in control over everything in the universe, does it then follow that *nothing* comes into our lives but what God has ordered? Or do bad things fit into the permissive will of God? Has God chosen to allow bad things to happen in our world and in our personal lives? We do know that God—in His sovereignty—chose to give humans a free will, as recorded in Genesis 2:16–17, which led to His creatures and His natural world becoming fallen.

These are weighty matters, and we will not know which side got it right until we find out in eternity. I expect that, because we will then be perfect, none of us will be tempted to say to those on the other side of the issue, "I told you so!" However, if we profess to love God it is a matter that we need to resolve for ourselves while we are creatures of this world, as it will determine our reaction and response to bad things that happen to us.

The answer to the question "Does God cause bad things to happen?" is an easy one when everything is going well in our lives, and that is that God is sovereign and rules over every aspect of our lives. But what about when something bad happens in our life? How then do we react and respond to the question?

## WHEN BAD THINGS HAPPEN

In his book *When Bad Things Happen to Good People* (originally published as *Why Bad Things Happen to Good People*) Rabbi Harold Kushner shares how he and his wife had to wrestle with the problem when a very bad thing came into their lives. He says that he and his wife were brought up to believe that God is all-wise and all-powerful and in control of everything in the universe. Until—yes, until—their son Aaron turned three. Aaron was a bright and happy child but was showing evidence of something being seriously wrong with his health. At eight months old he stopped gaining weight, and at a year old his hair fell out. Eventually Aaron was diagnosed with progeria (rapid aging). His parents were informed that their son would not grow beyond three feet tall, would never grow hair and would look like a little old man while still a child. As Rabbi Kushner asks, "How does one handle news like that?" And then Aaron's life came to an end at 14 years of age.

The rabbi and his wife handled it by changing their theological view of the relationship between God and bad happenings. They came to believe that there is such a thing as random acts of nature. It was just something that *happened* in their lives and was *not caused* by God.

## MY THEOLOGICAL TURNABOUT

And that is precisely what I had to do. For years I had believed, preached and taught that *everything* that happens in our lives (good and bad) comes directly from the hand of God, that they are always according to the will of God and that He planned them the precise way they happened. That's easy theology to accept when you have not had any experience with heartbreaking and heart-wrenching traumas that leave you in a state of shock, particularly when they are the result of unwise human behaviour. Did God *plan* that a young couple's three precious children and their grandmother would be killed in an automobile accident by a drunk driver?

## WHEN BAD THINGS HAPPENED TO ME

And what about when I was faced with watching my beloved wife struggle with a chronic health problem for 17 years and then pass away at the age of 47, leaving me with teenage sons? Marion was such a good person, who as a pastor's wife blessed untold numbers of people with her caring spirit and listening heart. Why her? Why not other Christian women her age, many of whom were living relatively self-centred lives? Would God *will* that to happen to Marion? Was it an *act of God?* Or is there a better explanation? I believe there is!

And what about when my beloved son was struck down with a rare virus (hemophagocytosis) that attacked his immune system—causing him and our family to suffer unbearable pain for five months—and then brought his earthly journey to an end at age 52? Kevin was such a good man, who like his mom blessed countless numbers of people with his light spirit and humorous approach to life. That was evident at his life celebration when person after person told me how Kevin had positively affected his or her life. And what about leaving his beloved wife a widow and his two wonderful sons without a dad? Did God *will* that to happen to Kevin? Was it an act of God? Or is there a better explanation? I believe there is!

And how does one apply the will of God to my beloved Carolyn's health situation? Such a sweet and caring person, with her life completely turned upside down, dealing with early Alzheimer's at age 65! Why her, while friends *her* age continue to go about living their normal lives and are still able to enjoy all the life skills that Carolyn has been robbed of? Skills like writing, reading, driving, cooking and baking, gardening, telephoning, planning ahead, completing a sentence, using a computer and dressing oneself, and the strength to go for a coffee or even a walk outside. Did God *will* that to happen to Carolyn? Was it an act of God? Or is there a better explanation? I believe there is!

## A VERY SAD STORY OF A MOTHER

Some time ago I got into a conversation with a lovely lady. As an icebreaker I had asked her how many children she had. That question quickly furrowed her brow and brought tears to her eyes. I immediately said I was sorry and perhaps she didn't want to talk about it. It's interesting (and lovely) how people will open up when they discover they are speaking to a minister. "No," she countered immediately, "I will share it with you." And what a story of pain it was! She had lost four of her six children, all at different times and through different circumstances. One of those was her only son, who was still in his twenties when he was killed by a drunk driver while riding his motorcycle. I was so glad that at that moment I remembered what my professor of pastoral psychology had taught us: There are occasions when a theological discourse is not appropriate, and neither are bromides. This was surely one of those occasions.

When I had regained my composure, I broke the silence by expressing how sorry I was and that I couldn't imagine the pain that those traumas had caused her. She then looked me in the eye and said, "I'm bitter! And I have quit going to church."

Well, how does a pastor respond to that one? I paused and then replied, "I'm sorry to hear that."

She then went on to explain the root of her bitterness. She had been taught in church that everything that happens to us is "according to the will of God" and that "God doesn't give us more than we can handle." Such erroneous teaching had caused her bitterness against God and was the reason she never wanted to enter the door of a church again, which has been the experience of many churchgoing people. I then assured her that I believed that those terrible things that happened to her had nothing to do with the will of God but were just *random acts of nature* and that she would be in my thoughts and prayers.

Sometime later I conducted a religious service in the facility, and there in the back row was this lady. After the service she said to me, "That's the first time I have been in church since the death of my son, and I enjoyed your service very much." It made me feel so warm that in some little way I got through to her.

## LEFT WITH TWO CHOICES

When we come face to face with trying to make sense of why heartbreaking, heart-wrenching situations happen to innocent and nice people, we are left with two choices: They are indeed all according to the will of God, and He not only allows them but *causes* them to happen, *or* there are other factors involved. The latter is what I now believe.

## FOUR FACTORS

I believe—after all these years of thinking and praying and reading about the subject—that every bad situation that happens in the world *apart* from those in which God shows forth His justice and holiness (for example, the flood) is a result of one of four factors:

1. Unwise behaviour of human beings (for example, being killed by a drunk driver)
2. Evil machinations of human beings (for example, 9/11)
3. Out-of-control natural phenomena (for example, the Thailand tsunami of 2004 that killed 250,000 people in a single day, left 1.7 million homeless and affected 18 countries)
4. Random acts of nature (for example, the illnesses that took the life of my beloved 47-year-old wife and my 52-year-old son and destroyed all the life skills of my beloved wife Carolyn)

## NO PLACE FOR BITTERNESS

As a result of my understanding of why bad things happen to good people, there has been no place in my spirit for bitterness. To be sure, I was and am deeply sorrowful that they happened to *my* loved ones and to *me,* but I am convinced that being *bitter* about them will not change them or make me a *better* person.

How my strong and vibrant faith made the difference is explained in part 2, chapter 1.

In the earlier stages of Carolyn's Alzheimer's and Parkinson's disease, she would often ask me if I believed that God had brought the disease into her life. Carolyn was brought up in a church—as I was—where they taught unequivocally that everything that happens in our lives is the will of God. That would mean that every vicissitude of our lives is *caused* by God. How glad I was to be able to assure her that God does not cause bad things to happen in our lives and then go on to explain that her illness belonged in the category of random acts of nature. I was also able to assure her—as I have assured many congregants during my pastoral ministry—that whatever happens to us in life, we can experience God's presence and peace. So, every evening after I get my beloved Carolyn ready for bed and tucked in, I pray with her and thank God for His presence and peace in both of our lives at this incredibly painful time we are going through together. With that, she closes her eyes and begins to fall off for a good night's rest and sleep, as promised in Psalm 127:2.

## RANDOM ACTS OF NATURE

Many people might be uncomfortable with the expression "random acts of nature." But how else do you explain the *good* fortune of some and the *bad* fortune of others in the same natural disaster? I lived in Barrie when the 1985 tornado ripped through the area. I was operating my decorating business at that time, and while the aftermath of the tornado was a goldmine for me and hundreds of other contractors, it was a devastating experience for hundreds of people. Six hundred homes were affected, with many destroyed. Eleven people died, including a nine-year-old boy riding home scared and as fast as he could on his bicycle. He was lifted off his bike and thrown against a house and died from his injuries. Why *him*? Why not some other family's child?

In church on Sunday, the congregants of course were abuzz with conversations about the tornado. A senior couple was praising God for His good favour in sparing their home, with only a little siding removed. However, another couple—usually at church with their three little children—was absent. Why? Because their house was not spared but totally destroyed. They were too distraught to be at church. The senior couple could have retreated to their condo in Florida if their house had been destroyed; the young family had to go to a motel.

Why the difference in the lives of these two couples? Why wasn't God's good favour bestowed on the couple with young children? The only sensible answer is that it was all a random act of nature. Otherwise, God would have to be accused of favouritism and malevolence, and that would be incongruous with His nature, so aptly described by the Psalmist: "*The LORD is compassionate and gracious... abounding in love*" (Psalm 103:8). And where is God in all these bad things that happen to us? He always turns up as "*our refuge and strength, a very present help in trouble*" (Psalm 46:1, KJV).

## Appendix 2
# DEATH'S STING "BE GONE!"

*"Where, O death, is your victory? Where, O death, is your sting?" The sting of death is sin, and the power of sin is the law. But thanks be to God! He gives us the victory through our Lord Jesus Christ.* (1 Corinthians 15:55–57)

It's an interesting fact of life that everyone knows they will die someday, but they're just not ready to talk about it yet. That is not how I feel about the subject. I have been blessed to live a wonderful and rich life, and I am ready anytime to complete my earthly journey and commence my eternal journey. I believe in two worlds: the world of flesh and blood and the world of the things of faith; the world of seen things (the physical world) and the world of unseen things (the spiritual world). The apostle Paul believed in those two worlds. When writing to his fellow believers at Philippi from his prison cell in Rome, while awaiting his possible execution for preaching the gospel, he said that he was of two minds. One was a desire to depart to be with Christ, and the other was a desire to remain so that he could continue to be a blessing to the Christians in Philippi (Philippians 1:20–24). That's what I call keeping life and death in their proper perspective!

## THE APOSTLE PAUL AND DEATH

If we summarized Paul's thoughts about death, what would that look like? Well, let's see what he has to say on the subject in his letters to the churches at Corinth and Philippi:

1. The bodies we are born with are not meant for eternity. He calls them an *"earthly tent"* (2 Corinthians 5:1). Paul knew the limitations of a tent, as he became a tentmaker in Corinth (Acts 18:3, 20:34).
2. Our bodies are going to be destroyed (2 Corinthians 5:1). Disease does just that!
3. While we are living in this earthly tent we will do a lot of groaning (2 Corinthians 5:2). (If you don't believe that, walk with me sometime through the halls of a long-term-care facility when I visit my wife.)
4. While *"we are at home in the body we are away from the Lord"* (2 Corinthians 5:6).

5. Paul's preference was to be "*at home with the Lord*" (2 Corinthians 5:8). That does not sound like someone who was afraid of death, dreading the thought of it or uncomfortable talking about it.

6. Paul looked upon death as something to be *gained*, something *far better* than continuing his life on earth (Philippians 1:21).

7. Paul was ambivalent about whether he wanted to go on living or die so that he could be in Christ's presence (Philippians 1:23).

8. The reason he desired to go on living was not to spend more time with his family and friends or go on more Christian cruises but to help the believers in the Corinthian church experience the fullness of joy in Christ that he experienced (Philippians 1:24–26).

9. Paul didn't look upon death as losing the battle or upon the end of his life on earth as a defeat. No, a thousand times no! Death to Paul was a victory over sin and death and hell (1 Corinthians 15:54–57)! Let me add here that no Christian should include in their obituary the words "After a long battle with…" That says that the battle was *lost*, when it was actually *won* by the fact of Christ's resurrection from the dead, and thus ours.

10. Paul believed that when Christ returns to set up His Kingdom on earth, believers will be given a new kind of body. The old is perishable, but the new will be imperishable; the old is weak, but the new will be strong; the old is a physical body, but the new will be a spiritual body; the old is like our parents' bodies, but the new will be like the body of our Lord Jesus (1 Corinthians 15:49).

11. Christ will transform our old bodies so that they will be like His "*glorious body*" (Philippians 3:21). That alone should help us to not put so much stock in these old bodies and thus to not have any dread or fear—*whatsoever*—about our death or, better put, the completion of our earthly journey and the commencement of our eternal journey. Yes, this is death without any sting! Thanks be to God!

12. Paul believed that even though our earthly body is comparable to a tent (speaking of its transitory nature), it is also comparable to a temple (speaking of the sacredness of its nature). In his letter to his fellow believers at Corinth he wrote, "*Do you not know that your body is the temple of the Holy Spirit who is in you, whom you have from God, and you are not your own? For you were bought at a price; therefore glorify God in your body*" (1 Corinthians 6:19–20, NKJV). I'm so glad that I was taught these truths in my youth, as they have become the primary motivation for me to live a healthy lifestyle (see part 2, key 5) and to glorify God through my body and in every way I can.

## DEATH IS CERTAIN

I think it is safe to say that the most loved, read and quoted psalm (and probably piece of literature) is the twenty-third psalm. In all the hundreds of memorial services (now often called celebration of life services) I have officiated at, a reading of this psalm will immediately bring a smile to the faces of all present. There is something so soothing, so assuring, so uplifting, so comforting about the whole tone of this spiritual poem. However, the Psalmist does not avoid the subject of the end of life but rather deals with it in a rather matter-of-fact manner. He states several important factors about death—or, as I prefer to refer to it, the completion of our earthly journey and the commencement of our eternal journey:

1. Death is certain. "*There is…a time to be born and a time to die*" (Ecclesiastes 3:1–2); "*Death is the destiny of everyone; the living should take this to heart*" (Ecclesiastes 7:2); "*It is appointed for men to die*" (Hebrews 9:27, NKJV); and "*Though I walk through the valley of the shadow of death*" (Psalm 23:4, NKJV).
2. Death does not have to be feared. "*Though I walk…I will fear no evil*" (Psalm 23:4). The valley of death will probably not be a pleasant place for most of us, but we have the assurance that our Shepherd is going to walk through it with us. He will be there to comfort us! Hallelujah! It is but a transition that will take us directly into the presence of our Lord (2 Corinthians 5:8).
3. Death—for believers in Christ—will transport us to "*an eternal glory that far outweighs*" all of our troubles (2 Corinthians 4:17). I believe that includes physical and psychological pain and suffering.
4. The fact of our certain death ought to give us serious thought about how we spend our lives. Moses prayed, "*Teach us to number our days, that we may gain a heart of wisdom*" (Psalm 90:12). I'm reminded of the maxim I learned in my youth: "Only one life, 'twill soon be past; only what's done for Christ will last."

## BETTER THINGS AHEAD

The apostle Paul wrote, "*Our citizenship is in heaven, from where we also wait for a Savior, the Lord Jesus Christ; who will change the body of our humiliation to be conformed to the body of his glory*" (Philippians 3:20-21, WEB*)*. Many of the hymn writers wrote about the fact of better days ahead.

Sanford F. Bennett wrote "In the Sweet By and By":

There's a land that is fairer than day
And by faith we can see it afar
For the Father waits over the way
To prepare us a dwelling place there.

In the sweet by and by
we shall meet on that beautiful shore
In the sweet by and by
we shall meet on that beautiful shore.

John Newton concludes "Amazing Grace" with this:

When we've been there ten thousand years
Bright shining as the sun
We've no less days to sing God's praise
Than when we'd first begun.

In my church youth group—many years ago—we loved to raise the roof with the singing of "Oh, That Will Be Glory," written by Chas. H. Gabriel:

When all my labors and trials are o'er
And I am safe on that beautiful shore
Just to be near the dear Lord I adore
Will through the ages be glory for me.

Oh, that will be glory for me,
Glory for me, glory for me,
When by His grace I shall look on His face
That will be glory, be glory for me.

Yes, says the apostle Paul (and it bears repeating), "'*Where, O death, is your victory? Where, O death, is your sting?' The sting of death is sin, and the power of sin is the law. But thanks be to God! He gives us the victory through our Lord Jesus Christ*" (1 Corinthians 15:55–56).

## THE BEST IS YET TO COME

People all age groups know something of the joy of anticipation, especially little children anticipating Christmas Day and their birthdays. The final book of the Bible—the book of Revelation written by the apostle John on the Isle of Patmos—draws back the curtain of eternity to give us a little glimpse of the glorious things that are ahead. In the final two chapters of the book John tells us of things that will be no more. God is going to make "*everything new*" (21:5), which means there will be no more death or mourning or crying or pain (21:4), no more night (22:5) and no more sin (22:3).

No wonder the apostle describes it as a time of great rejoicing, "*a great multitude in heaven shouting: 'Hallelujah! Salvation and glory and power belong to our God, for true and just are his judgments'*" (19:1–2). And the shouting of the multitude continued—sounding like the roar of rushing waters and loud peals of thunder—"*Hallelujah! For our Lord God Almighty reigns. Let us rejoice and be glad and give him glory!*" (19:6–7).

For those of us who have never had the pleasure of singing in a mass choir, we can anticipate that day when all of our voices will blend in harmony with the millions of the redeemed to praise our great God and our Saviour, the Lord Jesus Christ. Hallelujah! Yes, many people of faith who have never shouted out "Hallelujah" in the presence of others will be doing so on that great day. Surely we can say, "The best is yet to come!" Hallelujah!

## WE WILL MEET AGAIN!

When my eldest sister, Ellen, knew that she was fast approaching the end of her earthly journey and about to commence her eternal journey, she would say to me as I was winding down a visit with her, "Goodbye for now, my beloved brother Ernie, and if I don't see you anymore down here, I will be looking for you up there, where there is no night, no parting and no tears. Always remember that I love you." With that I would pray with her and then walk down the hall of the long-term-care facility with tears flowing down my cheeks, tears of sadness and yet of joy, knowing that indeed we would meet again.

## PERSONAL THOUGHTS ABOUT THE COMPLETION OF MY EARTHLY JOURNEY

1. I have absolutely no fear or dread of my end-of-life experience. Neither did the Psalmist, who wrote, "*Even though I walk through the valley of the shadow of death, I will fear no evil, for you are with me*" (Psalm 23:4, WEB). He then concluded the Psalm on an upbeat note: "*Surely your goodness and love will follow me all the days of my life, and I will dwell in the house of the* LORD *forever*" (Psalm 23:6).
2. As I move toward the conclusion of my earthly journey and the commencement of my eternal journey, it is my prayer that I will be able to echo what the apostle Paul wrote about his approaching departure from this world. To young Timothy he wrote, "*the time for my departure is near. I have fought the good fight, I have finished the race, I have kept the faith. Now there is in store for me the crown of righteousness, which the Lord, the righteous Judge, will award to me on that day—and not only to me, but also to all who have longed for his appearing*" (2 Timothy 4:6–8).

It has been my pleasure to have received many awards for my work with charitable organizations, such as the Rotary Club International Paul Harris Award for volunteer service, the Citizen of the Year Award from the city of Barrie, and the Honorary Life Chair of the Barrie and District Christmas Cheer organization. However, none of these awards will compare to the one I am anticipating receiving from my Lord and Saviour Jesus Christ when I appear before Him in eternity and receive that "crown of righteousness." I love the words of Jim Hill's song "What a Day That Will Be":

What a day that will be,
When my Jesus I shall see…
What a day, glorious day that will be!

# PRAISE AND WORSHIP

The Psalmist declares, *"Shout for joy to the L<small>ORD</small>, all the earth"* (Psalm 100:1). Note the emphasis here on our singing being joyful, not necessarily harmonious (although our human ears enjoy it more that way!) as God desires our songs of worship to be from our *hearts,* not just from our *voices.*

## CONGREGATIONAL SINGING

I have been intrigued by congregational singing since I was a little boy. My eldest sister, Ellen, told me that when we would arrive home from Sunday morning church and were waiting for the soup to heat up, I would stand up on the coffee table and call out hymns, just like the song leader did that morning. And of course my eight sisters (my brother hadn't been born yet) would go along with my performance. So congregational singing has been an integral part of my life for over 80 years. The Sunday Evening Gospel Hour (as it was called back then but is now a thing of the past), commenced with 20 to 30 minutes of an all-request hymn sing, sung with great enthusiasm with accompaniment by an organ and piano. I still love the combination of those two amazing instruments leading congregational singing. I carried on this practice all through the years of my pastoral ministry.

## THE APOSTLE PAUL AND CONGREGATIONAL SINGING

The apostle Paul was a strong believer in Christians coming together to sing songs of praise. He wrote, *"speaking [ministering] to one another with psalms, hymns, and songs from the Spirit. Sing and make music from your heart to the Lord, always giving thanks to God the Father for everything, in the name of our Lord Jesus Christ"* (Ephesians 5:19–20). Notice the emphasis here on *always* and *everything.* He is not advocating that we praise God *for* everything that happens in our lives—as that would be unrealistic—but he is admonishing us to praise God *in* everything, that is, whatever our circumstances may be.

Ernie Nullmeyer

Why does Paul speak of three categories of ministering to each other in our spiritual songs? What does he mean by differentiating between psalms, hymns and spiritual songs? I believe there are three reasons:

1. There are various styles of worship service songs. We need to take note of that!
2. One is not better than the other, although many Christians today believe that their preferred style is the "one and only."
3. All should be included in congregational singing, as Paul didn't use the conjunction "or" but rather the conjunction "and."

Through the years there have been many interpretations proffered as to what Paul meant by each of the three types of spiritual songs. My interpretation is as follows, for what it is worth: psalms are straight from the book of the Psalms in the Hebrew Bible, hymns are based on biblical truth, not directly from the Psalms, and spiritual songs are contemporary songs based on biblical truth but perhaps with a different beat.

However, the most important aspect of congregational singing is not the style or the tempo (allegro or adagio) or the level of the sound (although a reasonable decibel level should be practised) or the type of instrumental accompaniment but rather—as Paul points out—that we sing from the heart and to the glory of God. This is what matters to God, and thus I am sure that He desires that His people would stop making a big fuss about the externals.

## WHEN GOD DOESN'T LISTEN TO HIS PEOPLE SINGING

In the days of the prophet Amos, God declared to His people that He had no respect for the "*noise of [their] songs*" or "*the music of [their] harps*" and He would close his ears to them (Amos 5:21–24). Why was that? It had nothing to do with the sound level but rather was because their singing wasn't emanating from pure hearts. They had forgotten what their Scriptures taught, that only those who have "*clean hands and a pure heart*" can come into God's presence (Psalm 24:3–4). And that applies to our singing together.

They had also forgotten that God doesn't judge by external appearances but by what is in the heart (1 Samuel 16:7). God had commanded them to practice justice and holy living, but they had not been obedient. As a result, God said He didn't want any part of their singing or their instrumental music.

## A WIDE VARIETY OF CONGREGATIONAL SINGING

How the heart of God must be grieved in recent years that so many evangelical congregations have divided over the style, tempo and sound level of congregational singing! To divide over substance or doctrine is one thing, but to do so over style, tempo or sound level is evidence of our self-centredness; that is, it has to be our way or we're on our way to another church. It has become so prevalent that a term has arisen to describe it: "church shoppers and hoppers."

I believe it is wrong for us to judge the manner in which other Christians worship and particularly the manner in which they express praise to God in the congregational singing. During the years of my itinerant preaching ministry, I had the pleasure of worshipping with congregations that practised a very wide variety of congregational singing. That variety included the following:

1. Only hymns based on the psalms
2. Only great hymns of the faith—and all of the verses, even if it meant that lunchtime would be delayed, much delayed!
3. Primarily great hymns of the faith with a few contemporary hymns added
4. Only contemporary hymns, with a praise band

## HOW TO STOP DIVIDING CHURCHES OVER CONGREGATIONAL SINGING

1. Include a balance between the great hymns of the faith and contemporary hymns.
2. Remind older Christians that many of the hymns they sang in their youth were contemporary at that time.
3. Have a balance between styles and sounds of hymns sung.
4. Have the praise band accompany some hymns and the organ or piano accompany others, and occasionally sing a cappella, which is the norm in many Mennonite congregations.

Many problems in our individual lives, married lives and church lives can be resolved by practising balance in all things. A fruit of the Spirit is self-control, which should mean that when things are not done in the way I think they should be—or would like them to be—I will control the urge to prove that I (and only I) am right and that others are wrong. A lack of balance can lead to divisions in churches, and it has and will continue to do so, until we are ready to compromise in areas of church life like congregational singing. Divisions in churches do not bring glory to God!

## SINGING WITH ENTHUSIASM

I was preaching in a church where the praise band really whooped it up! As I sat on the platform enjoying the wonderful enthusiasm of the band members leading the congregational singing with joy, I could see many of the seniors in the pews looking anything but pleased with it all. I thought to myself that it was probably a matter of time until many of them would go church shopping and hopping. I found out later that unfortunately I was right. Yes, another church division! How sad! How wrong! How unnecessary, and all because of a lack of balance and a lack of wise pastoral leadership.

My former pastorate in Barrie—Emmanuel Baptist—is a congregation with a very large number of seniors and youth. Through wise leadership and the balance I have written about, seniors and youth enjoy together the congregational singing in the worship services. The seniors are blessed by the enthusiasm of the youth singing loud, fast and joyful songs such as "Mighty to Save," "Light of the World" and "Shout to the Lord," and the youth are blessed by the spirit of reverence expressed in more meditative great hymns of the faith such as "All the Way My Saviour Leads Me," and "Praise My Soul the King of Heaven."

## OLD COVENANT BELIEVERS AND ENTHUIASTIC SINGING

When older Christians find it difficult to accept the new style of singing hymns, they need to be reminded of what the Bible has to say about joyful outward expressive and even loud praises of Old Covenant believers. Allow me to present a few examples.

> *Shout for joy to the LORD, all the earth, burst into jubilant song with music; make music to the LORD with the harp, with the harp and the sound of singing, with trumpets and the blast of the ram's horn—shout for joy before the LORD, the King. Let the sea resound, and everything in it, the world, and all who live in it. Let the rivers clap their hands, let the mountains sing together for joy; let them sing before the LORD. (Psalm 98:4–9)*

Wow! Now that's a praise and worship event! Notice the verbs: "shout," "burst," "clap." Isn't that exactly what is happening among many of our Christian youth today? They feel enthused and excited about their life in Christ, and they don't want to hold it in, as many older Christians would like them to. Take note also of verse 1 of several psalms: "*Sing to the LORD a new song*" (Psalm 96:1, 98:1, 149:1). Isn't that a synonym for "contemporary"? Youth want something that is different, just as we seniors did when we were in our youth.

> *David told the leaders of the Levites [priests in charge of music in the temple] to appoint their brethren to be the singers accompanied by instruments of music, stringed instruments, harps, and cymbals, by raising the voice with resounding joy. (1 Chronicles 15:16, NKJV)*

Was this the first praise and worship band? The songs were to be joyful! While the harps were quiet-sounding instruments, the cymbals would be similar to our percussion today.

*"So David and the elders of Israel and the commander of units of a thousand went to bring up the ark of the covenant of the LORD from the house of Obed-Edom, with rejoicing"* (1 Chronicles 15:25–28). Note: they did it with rejoicing and with shouts and with very loud instrumental accompaniment: ram's horns, trumpets, cymbals, lyres and harps. Wow! What a hallelujah time that must have been! Imagine people of God getting *that* enthused and excited about spiritual things! I can imagine the judgment of some, labelling it fanaticism and commenting that the music was too loud.

Isn't it interesting that we can get excited about a six-ounce round black thing going into a net to determine the winner of the Stanley Cup or a five-ounce white round thing being hit over the fence (Joe Carter) to win the World Series, but to get that excited about the things of God for many Christians is just going too far. Could it be that God has raised up a new generation to show us older believers how praise and worship should be done? I am not, of course, advocating that worship services be turned into rock concerts, only that occasionally we sing songs of praise that cause us to show forth a little excitement for what we are singing about. "Praise my soul the King of heaven, to his feet thy tributes bring; Ransomed, healed, restored, forgiven, evermore his praises sing." Wow! Those are exciting words that we should sing with enthusiasm.

## THE HILLS AND THE TREES ALIVE WITH THE SOUND OF MUSIC

According to the Bible, life is to be filled with joy (in spite of the circumstances). The prophet Isaiah proclaimed to God's people of his day, *"You will go out in joy, and be led forth in peace; the mountains and hills will burst into song before you, and all the trees of the field will clap their hands"* (Isaiah 55:12). Note the outward emotion expressed here. Surely if the mountains can "burst into song" and the trees can join in clapping, we who have been redeemed should—at least on occasion and in spite of what the circumstances are in our lives—break forth into enthusiastic praise for all the wonderful blessings God so freely bestows upon us each and every day.

## SAVING THE BEST TO THE LAST

"Saving the best to the last" is a familiar statement to all of us and what I think was the criteria for placing Psalm 150 last in the psaltery. It is bookended with the admonition to *"Praise the LORD,"* and this admonition is repeated 13 times in six short verses, so we might justifiably conclude that the Psalmist got caught up in praising the Lord. I wonder if he would find that kind of spirit in many of our worship services these days.

The Psalmist goes on to develop that theme by telling us the following:

1. Where we should praise God: indoors ("*in his sanctuary*") and outdoors ("*in his mighty heavens*"). In other words, wherever we find ourselves, and in spite of the circumstances we may be going through, we should live in a spirit of praise.

2. What we should praise God for: His works of power, glory and majesty. Have we lost a sense of those three attributes of our great God, and in particular a sense of His majesty?

Some years ago when Carolyn and I were on a bus tour in Scotland, we had one of those always welcome staying-put days (which you will understand if you have ever been on a bus tour). It was a Sunday, so we decided to get up and go to a church within walking distance of our hotel. We received a very warm welcome, and the leader, accompanied by the praise and worship band, commenced the service with a hymn we had never heard before. It was called "Majesty" and was written by Jack Williams Hayford. The hymn seeks to elevate our thinking as to how majestic our God is. The Psalmist also sought to do this when he bookended Psalm 8 with these lofty words: "*LORD, our Lord, how majestic is your name in all the earth!*" (Psalm 8:1, 9). This indicates to me how "caught up" in his spirit he became when dwelling on the fact of God's majesty. The Psalmist also declared the greatness of God when he wrote, "*The LORD reigns, let the nations tremble; he sits enthroned between the cherubim, let the earth shake. Great is the LORD in Zion; he is exalted over all the nations. Let them praise your great and awesome name—he is holy*" (Psalm 99:1–3).

Partway through the hymn I found myself getting caught up in the spirit of the song. You might remember that the apostle John said that when he was on the island of Patmos (having been banished there by Rome for preaching the gospel), "*On the Lord's Day I was in the Spirit*" (Revelation 1:10). I found myself raising my hands, something we Baptists don't normally do in a worship service. Tears began warming my cheeks as I sang with the congregation and thought more deeply than I ever had about how majestic our God is! I felt overwhelmed with the thought that this God of majesty, the Creator of the universe, would be willing to give His only Son to die that I might become the person He desired and planned for me to be. Also, that He would reach down into a very ordinary, humble family of 12 (living in old rented houses in Toronto) and save me and call me to preach and minister to thousands of people. No wonder I felt so overwhelmed by God's majesty and grace!

Every day I continue to marvel as God continues to use me to be a blessing wherever I go.

## HOW WE SHOULD PRAISE GOD

The Psalmist continues his call to praise by moving from *where* we should praise God and *what* we should praise God for to *how* we should praise God (Psalm 150:3–5). We should praise God with seven instruments (seven being the number of perfection in Scripture) and all them blending to rise up into a mighty sound of praise to our mighty God! There is a wide variety of instruments in the orchestra: trumpet, harp, lyre, tambourine, strings and flute, clashing and resounding (reverberating) cymbals. Can you imagine it? It's a beautiful metaphor of how a congregation should work: a wide variety of people coming together to give forth a harmonious sound to the world. How sad that so often that is not the kind of sound non-church attenders hear coming from a congregation of believers.

As the Psalmist is coming to the conclusion of his call-to-praise poem, he seems to be running out of words as he gets caught up in a spirit of praise, so he concludes with a glorious admonition: "*Let everything that has breath praise the Lord*" (vs. 6)!

## A UNIFYING AND JOYFUL EXPERIENCE

Congregational singing through the years has been a unifying experience, not—as it is too often in this generation in so many congregations—a dividing experience. As we are one in Christ, brought together by the guidance of the Holy Spirit, it should not matter which hymnbook we sing out of or if a hymnbook is used at all or replaced by today's new technology to flash the words on a screen. Nor should it matter what instruments accompany the singing, as a wide variety is suggested in Psalm 150. What should be important is that when we join other believers in song, we are in tune with what God's Word teaches us about singing together as God's people. "*Come; let us sing for joy to the Lord; let us shout aloud to the Rock of our salvation. Let us come before him with thanksgiving and extol him with music and song*" (Psalm 95:1–2). "*Worship the Lord with gladness; come before him with joyful songs…Enter into his gates with thanksgiving and his courts with praise; give thanks to him and praise his name*" (Psalm 100:2–4).

## WHAT THE PSALMS TEACH US ABOUT CONGREGATIONAL SINGING

These calls to worship teach us that when we come together to sing praise to God, our songs should be the following:

1. Joyful: That's a spirit of congregational singing that Christian youth have brought into the church in this generation. We who are older should not shun it but embrace it and encourage it. Many of the older hymns of the faith that I was brought up on lack this emotion. "*Shout for joy to the LORD*" (Psalm 100:1).
2. To the Lord: We need to always keep in mind the purpose of our congregational singing; it should always be about God's glory, not about our likes and dislikes.
3. Passionate: Shouting for joy to the Lord is also encouraged in Psalm 66: "*Shout with joy to God, all the earth! Sing the glory of his name; make his praise glorious! Say to God, 'How awesome are your deeds!'*" (Psalm 66:1–3). The Psalmist even says, "*the hills are clothed with gladness*" and "*the meadows…and the valleys…shout for joy and sing*" at the awesomeness of God (Psalm 65:12–13). If the hills and valleys do it, why not His redeemed people?
4. Expressive of a thankful heart: "*Enter his gates with thanksgiving and his courts with praise*" (Psalm 100:4).

## OUR LORD'S HIGH PRIESTLY PRAYER

Our Lord in His high priestly prayer (John 17) prayed that His followers would "*be one as we are one*" (vs. 11) and that all future followers would also "*be one, Father, just as you are in me and I am in you*" (vs. 21).

Did our Lord mean that we should compromise our doctrinal beliefs and convictions?

I think not! There are certain cardinal truths declared in God's Word that we should not compromise on. However, as followers of Christ we need to learn to be willing to compromise on matters that are not clearly spelled out in the Word of God, such as congregational singing. In relating to one another as a Christian congregation, we should follow these principles:

> On the majors—adamant (doctrines)
> On the minors—acceptance (congregational singing, etc.)
> In all things—affection (which is what Jesus commanded!)

Jesus said to His disciples, and thus to us, "*A new command I give you: Love one another. As I have loved you, so you must love one another. By this everyone will know that you are my disciples, if you love one another*" (John 13:34–35). Our Lord didn't say that the proof of our discipleship would be what songs we sing in the worship service or how we sing them.

May God grant that congregational singing in all churches will be a uniting force that brings glory to God, not a divisive force that brings disrepute to His holy and glorious name!

## FACING THE INEVITABLE REALITY OF CHANGE

Many Christians today find it difficult (if not impossible) to change the way they think about congregational singing, but they forget that through the years they have made changes in many aspects of their lives. Change is a reality of life; no matter how much we like it or dislike it, change is simply going to happen! Children and youth love change, as they find it so easy to get bored, as every parent would attest to. However, as we age it becomes more and more challenging. In our senior years, we don't want to let go of the past, even though intellectually we understand that we have no choice. We get deeply ensconced in our comfort zone, and we don't want to be disturbed. I lived in a retirement residence for a period of time and found it fascinating how unhappy some seniors could be about having to change their residence and their lifestyle. By constantly thinking and talking about all that they had to give up, they caused themselves and their families unnecessary anxiety. I am blessed that I have always met change head on and put into practice my three "A" principles: Accept, Adapt, Advance. By letting go of the past we can move on into the future to experience new adventures and new joys. To be sure, any sudden change in our lives can create much deeper pain than if we had time to plan the change.

## CHANGE IN CONGREGATIONAL LIFE

The aversion to change that many people have can affect congregational life in many different ways. Someone has said that the seven last words of the church are "We have always done it this way."

When I commenced my ministry in Hamilton, I learned that there were congregants who believed that certain pews belonged to them and their families. When new people began to attend, they could find themselves sitting in a family pew. This could be very embarrassing for newcomers and difficult for the ushers to deal with.

I have always felt that situations like that can best be dealt with by using a little humour. So one Sunday during the announcements I mentioned how glad we were to see so many visitors attending our services, and so it would be important to remember that while we saved souls in this church, we did not save seats. It went over very well, and the old-timers got the message.

We all know the story of the lady who cut the Christmas dinner turkey in half to cook it in the oven. When asked why she did that, she responded, "Because my mom always did; you'll have to ask her." When the mother was asked, she responded, "Because Grandma always did; you'll have to ask her." Grandma was questioned, and she responded, "Because I didn't have a roasting pan large enough to hold the whole turkey."

## THE FIRST CENTURY CHURCH AND CHANGE

The first people who embraced the message of the gospel in the first century had to make dramatic changes to their concept of worship. Most of them were Jews and so attended worship on the Sabbath Day. Now, as Christians, they were gathering together on the Lord's Day (Matthew 28:1; Acts 20:7; 1 Corinthians 16:1–3). While they still continued to attend the temple services for prayers (at 9 a.m. and 3 p.m.), they also met together in houses for fellowship and the breaking of bread (Acts 2:42–47). What a contrast to worshipping in the grandeur of the temple! They also had to get used to the fact that many new people were coming to salvation in Christ (Acts 2:41, 5:14) and thus into their fellowship, which meant that the dynamic of the gathering would be altered dramatically and constantly. Luke tells us that in one day about three thousand people were baptized and added to the church (Acts 2:41). Can you imagine the adjustments the original group had to make? They also had to adapt to change in regards to their personal finances. *"All the believers were together and had everything in common. They sold property and possessions to give to anyone who had need"* (Acts 2:44–45; see also Acts 4:34–35). How would we as Christians today make *that* radical change in relation to our personal finances?

## CHANGE IN TIME OF WORSHIP SERVICES

From my childhood through to my pastoral ministry days, congregations who would label themselves as Evangelicals or Conservatives held two Sunday services, always at 11 a.m. and 7 p.m. The morning service centred on the theme of worship, while the evening service featured Gospel songs, music and a message, with an invitation usually given for people to respond to the message and receive Christ as Saviour.

Slowly—but surely—all that began to change. Evening services were discontinued as many changes were taking place in society. People seemed to be getting busier and were moving to the suburbs, which meant they had longer distances to drive to church.

More and more youth became disenchanted with church and so attended only occasionally, or not at all. We knew that youth were flocking by the tens of thousands to secular musical events where they could express themselves emotionally. Then came the rise of a new kind of Christian artist, like Amy Grant and Michael W. Smith, singing the same message that the church had always proclaimed—exalting Jesus as Saviour and Lord—but with a different sound and beat. This resulted in the rising up of what are now known as praise and worship bands, most of them made up of youth. Even Billy Graham's crusades began to include the new style of Christian music—along with long-time favourite and much-loved George Beverly Shea.

## YOUTH EMBRACE CHANGE

With the introduction of Power Point for lyrics, many congregations ceased using hymnbooks, which left worshippers' hands free to clap and raise during the singing. This was a radical change that many older Christians simply could not tolerate, which led to divisions. On the flip side, huge numbers of youth were no longer giving up on church when they reached their teens. They were remaining to become not just the "church of the future" but the "church of the present." It's inspiring to be in a worship service and witness youth expressing their faith and their deep love of Jesus in a new and different way than what I was brought up on. God must be smiling, even if a lot of His people are frowning.

I was preaching in a church in which a praise band was leading the congregational singing, and the youth were into it emotionally. When shaking hands on the way out, I said to one of the older congregants, "What do you think of the new style of sound of Christian music?"

With a twinkle in his eye he replied, "Pastor, it thrills my soul to see our youth expressing their faith in such a passionate way. They're just doing it in a different way than we did when we were that age." That's the spirit we need in our churches today among older Christians, a spirit that would prevent yet another division.

## OUTDOOR SUMMER SUNDAY EVENING CHURCH SERVICES

The first summer of my pastorate in Barrie (1953) was a scorcher, back in the days when very few buildings were air conditioned, and certainly not churches. During an evening service (and of course, back in those days, dressed in a shirt, tie and suit), I thought, *Why are we sitting here in an enclosed facility and wiping our brows when we could be holding our summer services in the great out-of-doors, enjoying the breeze and reaching people with the gospel whom we would never reach in an indoor service?* At the next meeting of the elders, I presented my idea of holding our Sunday evening services in a local park. Well, you would think I was suggesting that we invite dancers to perform at the service. I assured them that I would preach the same message "but using a different method."

Many questions were posed: "What about if someone dropped by the church and found it closed?" "How would we get the chairs set up?" "Could we get permission from city council?" "What would we do about setting up for the radio broadcast in a park?" All of these questions emanated from a dislike of change.

Then one deacon spoke up and said, "My brothers, God hasn't ordained that we hold our Sunday evening services inside a building; in fact, He hasn't even ordained that we should hold Sunday evening services. Our pastor just wants to get the gospel message out to more people and in more comfortable surroundings. Let's go ahead with it!" What a breath of fresh air! Here was a man with a vision. The Bible says, "*Where there is no vision, the people perish*" (Proverbs 29:18, KJV).

A motion was finally made that we move ahead with the change. We presented the motion to the church members, and all present approved it, believing— as I did—that God was in it! City council approved the use of the lovely St. Vincent Park on the shores of beautiful Lake Simcoe (the mayor was a member of our congregation). I have always believed in aiming for the best, and that was certainly the very best location in the area for our Sunday evening outdoor church services, which were also broadcast over the local radio station. Setup committees were appointed, and everything came together beautifully. Crowds came to witness this unusual church service—which I advertised on my "Good News" broadcast every Wednesday morning—and God blessed this new method of proclaiming the gospel, with many making a profession of faith in Christ. We conducted the park services for years, until I accepted a call to become pastor of Stanley Avenue Baptist Church in Hamilton.

One of the greatest sermons ever preached was in the great out-of-doors— on Mars Hill—by the apostle Paul (Acts 17). Many of Billy Graham's greatest crusades were held in the out-of-doors, some even in the rain (Wimbledon, London, England).

## OUTDOOR SUMMER SUNDAY EVENING CHURCH SERVICES IN HAMILTON

Interestingly, when I became pastor of Stanley Avenue Baptist Church in Hamilton and recommended—as I had in Barrie—that our summer Sunday evening services be held in a park, the elders expressed considerable discomfort about it. One of the main arguments was that the church doors had never been closed on a Sunday evening in the 100-year-history of the church. I was tempted to reply "So what?" but I restrained myself. Another argued that Hamilton city council had always been opposed to loudspeakers in any of the parks. And of course they would be a realistic necessity, even though I do have a powerful voice. I then suggested that we bring the matter before the congregation. We did, and they voted 100 percent to proceed with the idea.

Now the ball was in my court as to how to approach city council on the matter. Then the thought came to me, *Why not go to the top and approach the mayor of the city?* Mayor Vic Copps (yes, the father of well-known MP Sheila Copps) lived just around the corner from our church, and I had many conversations with him. We often had congenial discussions about spiritual matters, as he was a devout Roman Catholic. One day as I was arriving at the church, who should be walking by but the mayor? I greeted him and then asked if he had a few minutes. "Sure," he responded, "how can I help you?" I told him about our desire to hold our summer evening services in a park and asked him how I should go about it. He responded, "Which park would you like to hold them in?" Well, why not ask for the best, I thought, so I told him that my top choice would be Dundurn Park, which is on the bay and home of the famous Dundurn Castle. He said, "Reverend, leave that with me, and I'll get back to you on it." I silently said, "Thank You, Lord."

In about 10 days, I received a letter marked "From the Office of the Clerk." Sure enough, the letter said that our request had been granted. Once again I said, "Thank You, Lord. Now please lead me in all the other details that have to be worked out."

A major one was the PA system, as we needed a portable one that was powerful, in spite of my powerful preaching voice. It is said of the founder of Methodism, John Wesley, that his voice could be heard in the out-of-doors by fifty thousand people. However, he hadn't been competing with motorboats and highway traffic nearby, as I would be in Dundurn Park.

One day as I was shopping in downtown Hamilton, I walked by the Royal Theatre, which was being demolished because of its age and condition. It was built in 1913 back in the days of silent movies and later featured stars like Rudolph Valentino and Gloria Swanson. A little sign on the sidewalk said "All contents for sale" and then listed them in very small print. One of the items was a PA system. I ventured in—with dust flying everywhere—and met the superintendent.

I introduced myself as Reverend Ernest Nullmeyer of Stanley Avenue Baptist Church, which I'm sure didn't mean much to him. I then told him that I was interested in the PA system and what I wanted it for. He still didn't look all that impressed! I then asked him what he would take for it, and he said, "Three hundred dollars," which of course was a lot of money back in 1962. I knew it was of the Lord, so I gave him a small down payment and told him I would check it out with my board and get back to him. The secretary of the board contacted the elders by phone, and all agreed that we should go ahead with it, which we did. Wow! What an answer to prayer! Hudson Taylor, the founder of China Inland Mission, said, "God's work done in God's way will never lack God's supply."

We held the summer evening services in the park, with excellent crowds and people committing their lives to Christ, for nine years, until I accepted an invitation to become the conference director of Canadian Keswick Bible Conference.

## CHRISTIAN SONGS AND MY SPIRITUAL WELL-BEING

In bringing this appendix to a close, I need to emphasize the vital part that Christian songs have played in my life. As sporting activities have been the warp and woof of my physical well-being, so spiritual songs have been the warp and woof of my spiritual well-being. As I raise my head off the pillow first thing in the morning I hum hymns, and I continue to do so throughout the day until I lay my head back on the pillow at night. When I awake in the night, I hum hymns.

I can remember as a little boy in Sunday school enjoying singing songs like "Jesus Loves Me" and "Jesus Bids Us Shine."

In my youth I loved singing songs in our church youth group such as "Since Jesus Came into My Heart," "He Lives" and "Love Lifted Me!"

What a wonderful change in my life has been wrought
Since Jesus came into my heart
I have light in my soul for which long I have sought
Since Jesus came into my heart

Since Jesus came into my heart
Since Jesus came into my heart
Floods of joy o'er my soul like the sea billows roll
Since Jesus came into my heart
Rufus H. McDaniel

I was sinking deep in sin, far from the peaceful shore
Very deeply stained within, sinking to rise no more,
But the Master of the sea heard my despairing cry,
From the waters lifted me, now safe am I.

Love lifted me!
Love lifted me!
When nothing else could help,
Love lifted me.
James Rowe

My celebration of life (to be soon or not to be soon) will include some of my favourite hymns.

Blessed assurance, Jesus is mine!
Oh, what a foretaste of glory divine!
Heir of salvation, purchase of God,
Born of His Spirit, washed in His blood.

This is my story, this is my song,
Praising my Savior all the day long;
This is my story, this is my song,
Praising my Savior all the day long.
Frances J. Crosby

All the way my Savior leads me
Cheers each winding path I tread.
Gives me grace for every trial
Feeds me on the living Bread...

When my spirit, clothed immortal
Wings its flight to realms of day
This my song through endless ages:
Jesus led me all the way.
Frances J. Crosby

I love to tell the story of unseen things above
Of Jesus and His glory, of Jesus and His love...
I love to tell the story; it did so much for me
And that is just the reason I tell it now to thee.

I love to tell the story
'Twill be my theme in glory
To tell the old, old story
Of Jesus and His love.
Arabella K. Hankey

## SINGING WITH THE HEAVENLY THRONG

In the New Jerusalem, I shall sing with the throngs of heaven the "Song of the Lamb": "*To him who sits on the throne and to the Lamb be praise and honor and glory and power, for ever and ever!*" (Revelation 5:13).

And with that great multitude in heaven I'll sing, "*Hallelujah! For our Lord God Almighty reigns. Let us rejoice and be glad and give Him glory! For the wedding of the Lamb has come, and his bride has made herself ready*" (Revelation 19:6).

And then we will all join together in the "Hallelujah Chorus," and over and over we shall sing, "Hallelujah! Halleluiah! Hallelujah! Hallelujah! For the Lord God omnipotent reigneth! Hallelujah!"

## GETTING IN PRACTICE NOW

Through the years of my preaching ministry I tried to encourage Christians to get practised up for that great choir festival. I rehearse it every day in preparation for the real performance. I would like to encourage you to start practising today and to practice every day until we meet our Saviour—the Lamb of God—face to face and tell the story saved by grace. Hallelujah!

It is my hope and prayer that I shall go on singing the songs of faith until that day when I sing the new songs of faith in the presence of my Lord and Saviour Jesus Christ, with all the redeemed of the ages.

# LIVING HAPPILY EVER AFTER

As one who has officiated at hundreds of weddings and given premarital counselling to all of those couples, I feel somewhat capable of writing on this subject. Through the years I have tracked a great many of those marriage relationships, and I believe that there was a common thread running through all of the ones where the couples literally did live happily ever after. This does not mean that every moment of their marriage relationship was a happy one, as that would be totally unrealistic to my thinking. But, as I had the privilege and pleasure of being present for the 50th anniversary celebration of many of the couples whose weddings I had officiated at, I have to say that they all looked like happily married couples to me. Maybe my premarital counselling paid off. The common thread of which I speak was also why both of my marriages were relatively happy. I say *relatively* because it would be totally unrealistic to claim that there were not any bumps along the way. Of course there were, but these were dealt with in a mature manner, and we moved on.

I will elucidate on the common thread in due time, but first to some statistics on marriage in our society.

## ALARMING INCREASE IN MARRIAGE BREAKUPS
According to research by the Vanier Institute of the Family, Canada's divorce rate now stands at a whopping 40 percent.[26] This same report states that the top 5 reasons for divorce are as follows:

1. Different values and interests
2. Abuse—physical, emotional or verbal, or all three
3. Alcohol and/or drugs

---

[26] "Study finds 40 per cent of Canadian marriages end in divorce," *Maclean's*, October 4, 2010, http://www.macleans.ca/general/study-finds-40-per-cent-of-canadian-marriages-end-in-divorce/.

4. Infidelity
5. Career-related conflicts

## LEGITIMATE BREAKUPS

There are situations in a marriage relationship when I believe it is advisable to make a radical change. One of these is when the woman—sometimes the man—is being physically, emotionally or verbally abused. As a pastor, I have felt compelled to give that advice to the spouse being abused. I would give the same advice to a person in a relationship with someone with an alcohol, drug or sexual addiction. However, a divorce or separation should take place only after the individual with the problem has either refused to take counselling or taken counselling and not changed his or her behaviour.

According to Statistics Canada, "Of 2 million Canadians who went through a breakup between 2001 and 2006, approximately half were ending a marriage and the other half were dissolving a common-law relationship."[27] Sounds like the same percentage in each case, but since there were far fewer common-law couples than married couples in 2001, a higher percentage of common-law couples dissolved their relationship. One has to wonder what happened to the covenant the married couples made with each other on their wedding day. Those living together in a common-law arrangement remained together for an average of 4.3 years; those in a marriage relationship, an average of 14.3 years.

## WHY SO MANY BREAKUPS?

All of this brings us to the question that must be asked: Why are there so many more marriage breakups today than there were 60 years ago, when I was in the early days of my pastoral ministry? It's a great and important question, but the answer is not as simple as we may think at first. We need to be brutally honest (which is the only kind of thinking I entertain, as anyone who knows me will agree) in answering this question. The fact of the matter is that there were many marriages 60 years ago where it would have been better—at least for the woman in the situation—if the relationship had been dissolved. But back then, wives didn't have the independent financial security that at least 60 percent of wives have today, and there were no women's shelters for abused wives to flee to.

---

[27] Statistics Canada, Publication 11–402-X, http://www.statcan.gc.ca/pub/11–402-x/2011000/chap/fam/fam02-eng.htm.

## THE SO-CALLED GOOD OLD DAYS

We need to be careful when we talk about "the good old days" as if everything about them was good. It was not! Consider the way we treated challenged individuals—such as people with Down Syndrome—in past years, keeping them shut up in anything but acceptable institutions. Or think of the disgusting and repugnant freak shows that were once a highlight at the CNE (Canadian National Exhibition) in Toronto.

Think of the belief that was very prominent in some religious circles years ago (and still is in some today) that "*Wives [should] submit to [their] own husbands, as to the Lord*" (Ephesians 5:22). In too many marriages a literal and out-of-context interpretation of those words has led to a total domination of the wife, even sometimes to physical or sexual abuse. In my pastoral ministry I have witnessed that, and it isn't a pretty sight or easy to try to work out.

## THE COMMON THREAD IN A HAPPY, HEALTHY, HARMONIOUS MARRIAGE

What then is the common thread that I believe is the foundation upon which a happy, healthy, harmonious (triple-H) marriage is built? That foundation is clearly spelled out by the apostle Paul in his letter to his fellow believers in Ephesus. He wrote, "*Husbands, love your wives, just as Christ loved the church and gave himself up for her*" (Ephesians 5:25). Of course this principle is to be applied to wives also, but it appears that Paul thought that the initiative rests with the husband, and I believe that to be true! Jesus is our prime example and model of this truth, "*who Himself bore our sins in His own body on the tree, that we, having died to sins, might live for righteousness*" (1 Peter 2:24, NKJV).

In some marriages I have known, one of the spouses believed that he or she could get around this principle by giving good and expensive material gifts to his or her spouse. There is of course nothing wrong with giving nice gifts to our beloved, as long as we don't consider it a substitute for *giving of ourselves*.

## BEING A BLESSING TO OUR SPOUSE

This means that our marriage relationship should be built on the foundation of a desire and determination to be a blessing to our spouse in every way we can. As humans we all have five emotional needs: attention, acceptance, appreciation, affirmation, and affection. Men and women will either receive these from their spouse or be inclined to seek them from some other person. A marriage relationship is not just about having *our* needs met (sexual or otherwise) but rather is about meeting the needs of our beloved. Solomon wrote, "*My beloved is mine, and I am his*" (Song of Solomon 2:16) and "*I belong to my beloved, and his desire is for me*" (Song of Solomon 7:10). I believe and know that a wife will respond to that love just as we have responded to the outpouring love of Jesus: "*We love Him because He first loved us*" (1 John 4:19, NKJV). The result will be a beautiful, fulfilled, Christ-exalting marriage! It will also result in both the husband and wife submitting to one another, but *always* in love, and an intimacy in the marriage that will be *completely satisfying to both wife and husband.*

## NECESSITY OF A SOLID FOUNDATION

Jesus taught us the importance of a solid foundation in His parable of the two men who decided to build a house. The unwise man built his house on the foundation of sand, and when the rains came down, the streams rose, the winds blew and beat against that house, and it crashed! But the wise man built his house on the rock. The rains came down, the streams rose, the winds blew and beat against that house, and it did not fall (Matthew 7:24–27).

### The House That Withstood the Storm

In July 1996, the region of Saguenay-Lac-Saint-Jean, Quebec, was covered in water from heavy rains, and entire neighbourhoods were swept away, with 10 residents losing their lives. But one house stood firm! While neighbours' houses were carried away by the torrents, a small white house withstood the unrelenting elements. Every tourist to the area wants to know how *this* house could stand while *all others* were swept away. The grandson of the owner—who established the house as a tourist attraction—answered that there were two explanations: one spiritual, the other scientific. The spiritual one had to do with his grandmother's prayer as she was being evacuated, a prayer that God would preserve her home. The scientific one was that the builder of the house in 1950 anchored the foundations right down to the rock.

## THE SOLID FOUNDATION IN A TRIPLE-H MARRIAGE RELATIONSHIP

Yes, our salvation is secure when it is built on the rock of the finished work of Christ on the Cross, and likewise our marriage is secure when we build it on the rock of giving ourselves up for each other. We do this not just because we are admonished by Paul to do so but because we love each other with everything that is in our being. On our 25th wedding anniversary, my beloved Carolyn gifted me with two lovely bird figures with the notation on the card "Lovebirds

Forever." How wonderful to be in a marriage relationship in which we are still lovebirds and continue to show that in warm and intimate ways, even in spite of her situation with Alzheimer's. Often when I am pushing her in her wheelchair around the halls of the long-term-care facility where she lives, one of volunteers will say, "Here come the lovebirds." What a beautiful (and true) compliment! That's an excellent segue to talk about sex in marriage.

## SEX IN MARRIAGE

As followers of Christ, we must determine—in a sexually saturated society—how we will face the fact of our God-given sexuality. What does the Bible say to us on the matter? As a starter, let me present a quote from Jesus: "*You have heard that it was said, 'You shall not commit adultery.' But I tell you that anyone who looks at a woman lustfully has already committed adultery with her in his heart*" (Matthew 5:27–28). Notice that Jesus doesn't say it is a sin to *look* at attractive women.

Years ago our family was out for a drive, and a rather attractive-looking lady walked by. Marion said to me, "Were you looking at that beautiful woman?"

Our son Kevin, about eight at the time and always quick with a quip, blurted out, "Mom, Dad is not dead yet! He was just *looking*!"

No, it is not a sin to look, but that can become the slippery slope to lusting in fantasy for that woman. If we men desire to be good witnesses for our Lord and Saviour Jesus Christ, we must always be on our guard as to how Satan works to bring us down and to bring reproach to the name of our Lord. The Bible has some powerful things to say about keeping our minds and lives pure:

> *The body...is not meant for sexual immorality but for the Lord...Flee from sexual immorality...Do you not know that your bodies are temples of the Holy Spirit, who is in you, whom you have received from God? You are not your own; you were bought at a price. Therefore honor God with your bodies.* (1 Corinthians 6:13–20)

> *Be alert and of sober mind. Your enemy the devil prowls around like a roaring lion looking for someone to devour. Resist him, standing firm in the faith.* (1 Peter 5:8–9)

When I was a boy in Sunday school we sang a song that in hindsight doesn't seem very appropriate for children to be singing, but it does present a powerful message to us all:

Yield not to temptation, for yielding is sin
Each vict'ry will help you some other to win
Fight manfully onward, dark passions subdue
Look ever to Jesus; He'll carry you through.

Ask the Savior to help you
Comfort, strengthen, and keep you
He is willing to aid you
He will carry you through
Horatio R. Palmer

## WHY MEN FEEL THEY HAVE A RIGHT TO SEXUALLY ASSAULT WOMEN

The media regularly presents stories of women being sexually assaulted, often in the workplace and too often by professionals and high-profile individuals. What is it that drives some men to lower themselves to this kind of repulsive, abhorrent behaviour? The answer is, they do not have a proper concept of what a sexual relationship should be about. It is not about thinking of a woman as an *object* to be desired but rather a natural result of two people committed in a marriage relationship who truly love each other.

## THE BIBLE AND SEXUAL RELATIONS

After God created Adam and gave him a suitable companion, the man said, "*This is now bone of my bones and flesh of my flesh; she shall be called 'woman,' for she was taken out of man*" (Genesis 2:23). The account goes on to say, "*That is why a man leaves his father and mother and is united to his wife, and they become one flesh. Adam and his wife were both naked, and they felt no shame*" (Genesis 2:24–25). We then read, "*Adam made love to his wife Eve, and she became pregnant and gave birth to Cain*" (Genesis 4:1).

So what does all this teach us about sexual relations in a marriage?

1. God initiated and ordained the concept of sexual relations between a man and a woman as husband and wife. "*[God] brought her to the man*" (Genesis 2:22).
2. Because God was involved in His creatures coming together in a sexual relationship, the experience is a *sacred* one. We live in a society in which sex has too often been portrayed as nothing more than a *physical* experience, whereas it is a wonderful sacred gift from God!
3. A man and woman are to *leave* their parents and *cleave* to each other. Of course this does not mean that they will not keep a close relationship with their parents, but it does mean—and better mean—that it is no longer on the same level that it was before they made their marriage vows. As a pastor I have witnessed husbands and wives (usually wives) trying to maintain a premarital relationship with their parents, and it destroyed the marriage. My advice was always "There are secrets between a husband and wife that should not be shared with anyone, and that includes one's parents, family and friends." An exception of course is when and if it becomes necessary to do so with a marriage counsellor. My advice to parents is "Never probe for information. If your married child wants you to know certain information, he or she will share it with you."
4. Sexual relations in a marriage is a very intimate experience: "*Adam and his wife were both naked, and they felt no shame*" (Genesis 2:25). This special relationship of intimacy in a marriage is what makes it all so beautiful.

5. Children are God's plan for the perpetuity of the human race, through a relationship between a husband and his wife.

6. No other human relationship should be as close as the relationship of husband and wife. When we refer to our "best friend," it should mean our spouse. In marriage we become soulmates; it is a union of not only our bodies but also our spirits and souls.

## THE RELATIONSHIP OF SEX AND AFFECTION

In a general sense men crave sex and women crave affection. This can lead to a problem in a marriage relationship. There's a statement that puts it well: "Men give affection to get sex, whereas women give sex to get affection." Women, in general, do not want a vertical expression of affection to always lead to a horizontal expression of sex.

If a married couple keeps the emphasis on expressing *affection* rather than on *sex*, they can have an intimate relationship with each other long after they are beyond extending their intimacy into a sexual act. This means that husbands—in particular—need to change their concept of intimacy. Often when married couples are counselled on the matter of their sex life, the wife will share that she would just like to be intimate or to express affection without it leading always to the bed.

## ON A VERY PERSONAL NOTE

Often in our private moments together in the long-term-care facility where Carolyn is living, she will say, "Just give me a hug" or "I just want you to hold me." What a joy to be still expressing affection to one another, knowing of course that it will not and cannot result in the sexual act. This joyful experience of expressing the pleasure of intimacy in our relationship will go on until death parts us.

When my son Brad was a little boy he was entertaining himself at something in our kitchen and noticed that Marion and I—while preparing the meal together—were expressing affection to each other. Brad looked up and said, "Daddy, I think you and Mommy should get married." Of course we were married but still expressing affection.

When our son Eric was packing up to go to Kitchener to prepare for his forthcoming wedding day, he said to Carolyn, "Mom, how many hugs do you and Dad have in a day?" His mom responded, "Oh, Eric, too many to count!" I believe that the greatest example that a couple can give to their children of what a loving marriage is all about is expressing affection to each other—in an appropriate way, of course.

I have this advice for all husbands: Concentrate on the affection aspect of your marriage relationship, and you will be delighted by how it will often lead to amazing and joyful sexual experiences. When it doesn't, revel in the joy of just expressing affection.

In a letter to his protege Timothy, the apostle Paul stated that God "*gives us richly all things to enjoy*" (1 Timothy 6:17, NKJV). This enjoyment should include the sexual relationship that a husband and wife have with each other and also their lifetime of expressing affection to each other.

## TWELVE TIPS TO BUILD A HAPPY, HEALTHY, HARMONIOUS MARRIAGE

While the foundation of a "triple-H" relationship is the giving of ourselves to our beloved soulmates, there are other factors involved in building that kind of relationship. These include the following:

1. Always express affection to each other.
2. Be true to the covenant-commitment made to each other on the wedding day. That means that you will love and cherish each other—in sickness as well as in health—"till death parts us."
   When I'm visiting Carolyn in the long-term-care facility (as I've done over 1,000 times since she was admitted), people will often say to me, "You're such a devoted husband." I suppose they mean that I am there for my beloved in spite of her speech problems and many other problems. I often feel like saying, "She ain't heavy; she's my beloved," to paraphrase the song. It helps of course that every time I visit with Carolyn she tells me how much she loves me and appreciates everything I do for her.
3. Be completely open with and accountable to each other. The apostle Paul writes, "*Speak truthfully*" (Ephesians 4:25). A marriage relationship built on secrets or deception will eventually fall apart, as the truth always gets out. There are many illustrations of that in the media with high-profile people. God laid down this principle in Numbers 32:23: "*You may be sure that your sin will find you out.*"
4. Practice forgiveness and thus don't hold grudges. Paul writes, "*Forgiving each other, just as in Christ God forgave you*" (Ephesians 4:32) and "*Get rid of all bitterness, rage and anger, brawling and slander, along with every form of malice*" (Ephesians 4:31). There's a popular song entitled "Hard to Say I'm Sorry," and we all know that is true! But there is no way around it if we are to have a happy, healthy, harmonious marriage and one that will last. When our beloved feels hurt about something we have said or done, the sooner we say we are sorry, the easier it will be, and the more respect our spouse will have for us. My advice is "Just do it!" And "Immediately!" Paul writes, "*Do not let the sun go down while you are still angry*" (Ephesians 4:26). It's okay and natural to get angry, but get it over with quickly, not allowing it to build up until it becomes a grudge.
5. Build up and don't ever belittle your spouse, particularly in public. It makes me sad when I hear a spouse speak disparagingly about their spouse in public! I have witnessed spouses breaking down and crying when their spouse has put them down in public. Paul writes, "*Do not let any unwholesome [hurting] talk come out of your mouths, but only what is helpful for building others up according to their needs, that it may benefit those who listen*" (Ephesians 4:29). Do not be like the husband who asked his wife why she kept buying so many hats. Her answer was "Every time I get down in the dumps, I pick one up." "Oh," said the husband, "so that's where you've been getting them." No hats off to him!

6. Be *dependent* on each other while also being *independent*. Have your own life! Do not allow your life to be controlled by a control freak. Do not try to meet all the needs of your spouse, as that is unrealistic and unattainable!

7. Do caring deeds for each other every day, without having to be asked or prodded, and do them *cheerfully*. If both spouses are going out to work, household duties must be shared; and if children are involved, those responsibilities *must also be shared*.

8. Have fun together. Of course it's important to pray together and to have a spiritual dimension to the relationship—but God has also made us to enjoy life, and that should include our marriage relationship. Blessed is the couple who laugh often together! Play table games; go out to movies, plays, concerts, sporting events, and for coffee; and don't forget dinners, even if it's only at McDonalds. And of course, have fun in bed, even if it's only a cuddle. Such pleasure! And what a way to fall asleep for a good night's rest and sleep and to awake in the morning with a "Good morning, my sweetheart!"

9. Never cease courting! When I did premarital counselling I would tell each couple that I could summarize in three words how they could keep the spark in their marriage. That piqued their attention! The three words? Never stop courting! If you held hands when courting, do it in marriage; if you said kind and loving things to each other when courting, keep saying them in marriage. Don't be like this husband and his behaviour before and after marriage:
Before Marriage: They walk along the street.
She slips.
He says, "Careful, sweet."
After Marriage: They walk along the selfsame street.
She trips.
He says, "Don't be so clumsy; pick up your feet."
If you did kind and loving deeds for each other when courting, do them in marriage. If you gave each other undivided attention (remember when you used to look longingly and lovingly into each other's eyes when sharing a milkshake?), keep doing it. Turn off your cellphones when you're with each other! The result will be that it will be truly said of your marriage relationship "They lived happily ever after!"

10. Complement each other. Each of you has strengths, and each has weaknesses. Accept your spouse for *what* they are and *who* they are. They did not marry you for you to try to make a different person out of them. If you try, you will only fail! Each of us has our own idiosyncrasies, and they are not going to change, no matter how much we are nagged about them! It has been said that "To every weakness there is a strength." Learn to enjoy and celebrate each other's differences and to become the strength where the other one is weak.

11. Compliment each other. I have already written about speaking words that put one's spouse down (number 6). Here I want to want to emphasize the importance of speaking words that will build one another up (Ephesians 4:29). It takes so little to make a person smile, make a person feel better about himself or herself, lift a person's spirit.
Years ago in one of my sermons I mentioned to the congregation that just before we were leaving the house to go to church, I turned to my wife and said, "My, you look beautiful!" At the end of the service while I was shaking hands with people as they left, wife after wife said to me, "Pastor, I wish *my* husband would compliment me once in a while." It's sad that wives should have to express that! However, husbands too need a complimentary word spoken to them by their wives once in a while. Even now when Carolyn's vocabulary is limited, she will say to me, "You look nice."

12. Keep a spiritual dimension in the relationship. While the song says "We Were Made for Each Other" (and that is good), we were also made to have an intimate relationship with God through our Lord Jesus Christ and the Holy Spirit. In my youth, wall plaques depicting Bible verses or maxims of various kinds were very

popular in Christian homes. I remember well one that was on a hallway wall near the entrance to our home. It said, "Christ is the Head of this home. The unseen guest at every meal. The silent listener to every conversation." How different many homes would be if they would take those statements seriously.

If you, my dear reader, are in a marriage relationship, may it be everything you desire it to be and everything God can make it to be. It takes work, dedication and passion, but it is—believe me—worth it! It pays great dividends. Amen.

## A BIBLE ACCOUNT OF INTIMACY

A chapter on the subject of marriage should not end without a reference to the biblical book Song of Solomon. Many biblical expositors interpret the book as a type of the love that Christ has for His Bride—the Church—and it *can be* so interpreted. However, there are too many references in the book to ignore the fact that it is really a beautiful story of the intimate relationship that a husband and wife should have with one another.

One of my elderly parishioners told me that he couldn't bring himself to read the book, because he thought there was too much about sex in it. Sad! It certainly isn't a part of Scripture that you would read when having family devotions. However, it is part of what we refer to as the Inspired Word of God, and it should be read as a love song and cause us to see sex on the level that God intended it to be.

## WHERE VICTORIANISM WENT ASTRAY

Victorianism caused people of faith to look upon sex with prudishness, and that resulted in a hindrance to the dissemination of some basic information on health and hygiene. In my youth, parents never—and I mean never—referred to private body parts by their proper names. The result was that those parts were given identities that were naughty at the least.

I had no idea what was happening in our home with my sisters on a monthly basis. It was all hushed up. I had to get my information from my friends in high school; there was no use asking my church friends, as their parents too never discussed such matters with them. I decided that when I became a parent, all parts of the body would be given their proper name, and I did so when bathing my boys. The subject of sex was treated as sacred but always with openness. I wanted my sons to be informed properly on the subject so that when they heard nonsense about it in the schoolyard they would feel proud that their dad had given them the *real* facts.

Prudery also led to people downplaying the enjoyment of sex and the liberty that a husband and wife should feel when expressing their love for each other at the deepest level. One of my college professors in a talk he gave annually to the male students made it clear that he believed that the sexual experience in marriage should be strictly for the purpose of procreation. That got a few smiles from the students. That is certainly not the impression we get from reading Song of Solomon.

In my marriage counselling sessions, I discussed the subject of sex in marriage with frankness, and couples always thanked me for the advice, as most of them had never heard anything like that from their parents. Sad! Is it any wonder that sex education has become a part of today's elementary school curriculum?

In a sex-saturated society, our youth need the facts that too many parents have not been sharing with their children. It is not just important but imperative that our youth know the real facts.

## A LOVE SONG ABOUT INTIMACY IN MARRIAGE

That is what the Song of Solomon is all about. It describes in frank terms what intimacy in a triple-H marriage should be like. The bridegroom refers to his bride as "my lover" and "my darling" and to parts of her body in glowing terms. Likewise, the bride refers to her bridegroom as "my lover," "handsome," and "charming." Wow! No wonder she says that their bed is "*verdant*" (flourishing) (Song of Solomon 1:16). One gets the impression that their love for each other can only be described as full abandonment to one another in mutual satisfaction. How beautiful!

## A METAPHOR OF OUR RELATIONSHIP TO OUR HEAVENLY LOVER

As we read in the Song of Solomon about the rapturous delight the bridegroom and bride experience, it becomes a magnificent and beautiful description of a redeemed sinner's relationship to the One who has made us His "bride." Yes, "*For God so loved the world that he gave his one and only Son, that whoever believes in him shall not perish but have eternal life*" (John 3:16) and "*We love because he first loved us*" (1 John 4:19) and "*Husbands [and wives], love [each other], just as Christ loved the church and **gave himself up for her**" (Ephesians 5:25, emphasis added). That's the common thread of a triple-H marriage: healthy, happy, harmonious!

# FINAL WORDS

My closing words of the book are those written by my most loved hymn writer, Fanny Crosby, who went blind at an early age and yet didn't allow that traumatic experience to keep her from becoming a mission worker and a composer of over 8,000 hymns. Two of my favourites sum up the story of my life.

This is my story, this is my song
Praising my savior all the day long.

To God be the glory!
Great things He has done!

I live in amazement that God could take a very ordinary person like me, coming from a very ordinary family, and bless his life and ministry in a very extraordinary way. Yes, indeed, the glory does belong to God, and to God alone!

However, it is my desire that the final words of this book should not be my words but the words of my Lord and Saviour Jesus Christ, as He speaks words of solace and comfort to all of our hearts:

*"Therefore I tell you, do not worry about your life, what you will eat or drink; or about your body, what you will wear. Is not life more than food, and the body more than clothes? Look at the birds of the air; they do not sow or reap or store away in barns, and yet your heavenly Father feeds them. Are you not much more valuable than they? Can any one of you by worrying add a single hour to your life? And why do you worry about clothes? See how the flowers grow. They do not labor or spin. Yet I tell you that not even Solomon in all his splendor was dressed like one of these."* (Matthew 6:25–29)

*"Do not let your heart be troubled. You believe in God; believe also in me. In my Father's house are many rooms; if that were not so, would I have told you that I am going there to prepare a place for you? And if I go and prepare a place for you, I will come back and take you to be with me that you also may be where I am."* (John 14:1–3)

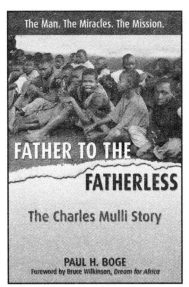

## *Father to the Fatherless*
by Paul H. Boge
ISBN 978-1-897213-02-5 Soft Cover
ISBN 978-1-894860-71-0 E-book
240 pages, size 6x9 Retail $18.95

## *Hope for the Hopeless*
by Paul H. Boge
ISBN 978-1-927355-03-9 Soft Cover
ISBN 978-1-927355-04-6 E-book
320 pages, size 6x9 Retail $19.95

## *Faith, Life & Leadership*
by Marg Gibb
ISBN 978-1-927355-81-7 Soft Cover
ISBN 978-1-927355-82-4 E-book
160 pages, size 6x9 Retail $19.95

## *Bent Hope*
by Tim Huff
ISBN 978-1-927355-81-7 Soft Cover
ISBN 978-1-927355-82-4 E-book
160 pages, size 6x9 Retail $18.95

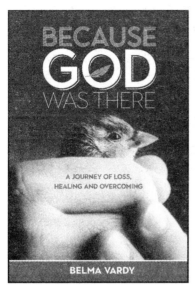

## *Because God Was There*
by Belma Vardy
ISBN 978-1-927355-85-5 Soft Cover
ISBN 978-1-927355-86-2 E-book
260 pages, size 6x9 Retail $19.95

## *Leading Me*
by Steve A. Brown
ISBN 978-1-927355-68-8 Soft Cover
ISBN 978-1-927355-69-5 E-book
176 pages, size 6x9 Retail $17.95

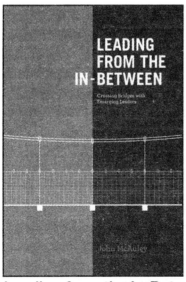

## *Leading from the In-Between*
by John McAuley
ISBN 978-1-927355-56-5 Soft Cover
ISBN 978-1-927355-57-2 E-book
112 pages, size 5.5x8.5 Retail $16.95

## *But If Not*
by Brenda Pue
ISBN 978-1-927355-79-4 Soft Cover
ISBN 978-1-927355-80-0 E-book
256 pages, size 6x9 Retail $19.95